KENNETH LONERGAN

Kenneth Lonergan was born in New York City in 1962. Plays include *This Is Our Youth* (The New Group, 1996), *The Waverly Gallery* (Promenade Theatre, 2000), *Lobby Hero* (Playwrights Horizons, 2001), *The Starry Messenger* (The New Group, 2009), *Medieval Play* (Signature Theatre, 2012) and *Hold on to Me Darling* (Atlantic Theater Company, 2016).

Work for the cinema includes *You Can Count on Me* (2000), *Gangs of New York* (co-written with Jay Cocks and Steve Zaillian, 2002), *Margaret* (2011) and *Manchester by the Sea* (2016). He also adapted E. M. Forster's *Howards End* for the BBC in 2017.

Awards include the Academy Award for Best Original Screenplay and BAFTA Award for Best Original Screenplay for *Manchester by the Sea*; the Sundance Film Festival Grand Jury Prize and Writers Guild of America Award for Best Original Screenplay for *You Can Count On Me*; while *The Waverly Gallery* was a finalist for the 2001 Pulitzer Prize for Drama.

T0347191

A Nick Hern Book

The Starry Messenger first published in Great Britain as a paperback original in 2019 by Nick Hern Books Limited, The Glasshouse, 49a Goldhawk Road, London W12 8QP

The Starry Messenger copyright © 2019 Kenneth Lonergan
Introduction copyright © 2019 Kenneth Lonergan

Kenneth Lonergan has asserted his right to be identified as the author of this work

Cover design: feastcreative.com

Designed and typeset by Nick Hern Books, London
Printed in the UK by Mimeo Ltd, Huntingdon, Cambridgeshire PE29 6XX

A CIP catalogue record for this book is available from the British Library

ISBN 978 1 84842 876 8

Kenneth Lonergan

THE STARRY MESSENGER

NICK HERN BOOKS
London
www.nickhernbooks.co.uk

Found in Space
Kenneth Lonergan

The original New York Hayden Planetarium was built in 1935 and demolished in 1997. That's about average for the lifespan of a beautiful, functioning building in New York, a city that tears itself down every twenty years or so, usually for reasons that have more to do with greed than need. One thing about the continual replacement of what need not be replaced is that what was valuable in the past is not built upon but lost.

I was a kid in the 1960s, the first great era of space exploration. The TV shows, movies, toys, board games, comic books, popular magazines and news programmes were dominated by the Space Race, by NASA, and by what appeared to be the fusion of science and science-fiction, finally meeting in the real world. Science, with its textbooks and experiments and demands of exactitude, had always seemed so dull compared to science-fiction, with its aliens and ray-guns. But suddenly it was science that seized the country's imagination, science that was sending people into space, and science that landed real live astronauts on the surface of the moon. When you watched the rockets go up on television you felt like the whole world was watching too.

A lot of what I saw was hard to understand. We would sit in front of our Zenith color TV through the interminable countdowns, watching the rows and rows of NASA scientists and engineers, with their crew cuts and white short-sleeved shirts and dark narrow ties, their cigarettes and headsets, sitting behind impossibly wide banks of controls and consols, and monitors which flickered in their faces inside the flickering light of the TV. It was a peculiar feeling to realize that these unexciting, profoundly ordinary grown-ups were behind the unbelievable excitement of space travel.

Before its popularity waned, the Planetarium was for many New York kids a place where the same excitement and lift of the imagination was made manifest in the realm of appreciable reality.

Its modest scale spoke somehow to the modest scale of our own Earth, just as the dome on which the Planetarium's stars were projected every afternoon and evening, during the Sky Shows, seemed to reflect the enormity of a world beyond our own, which most of us couldn't really imagine, let alone begin to understand.

Inside the Planetarium it was made clear to us that if we are unable in the end to grasp the full extent of the universe around us, it will not be on account of anything that lies beyond the limits of physical reality, but because physical reality itself extends beyond what the human mind, extraordinary as it is, may be able to conceive. Equally daunting, however, and inspiring, was the story of how far we have gone toward penetrating those mysteries, and the oddly pedestrian character of the work involved in the attempt.

These were immensely exciting and powerful ideas. Because the old Planetarium, with its rotating mechanical ceiling model of the Solar System; its huge mounted meteorites, smoothed and pitted by the heat generated when they ploughed through atmosphere, which you could run your hands over without being asked to step away from the exhibit; its really beautiful projected Sky Shows; and even the toy spacemen and rocket-shaped pencil erasers in their 1960s cardboard packaging, available in its gift shop; all these things spoke to the mind-blowing idea that the universe is not imaginary.

Business fell off badly in the '80s and '90s, until the Museum of Natural History, to which the Planetarium belonged, rejuvenated itself by reconfiguring its famous dinosaur exhibits and demolishing the old Planetarium in favor of a new structure which, while it improved on the technology, lost everything in the presentation, and in what was being presented.

When the old Planetarium was destroyed, something much bigger was destroyed along the way; in the notion of science as something thrilling on its own terms; of science as part of the zeitgeist; of the availability of science to everyone; of the enormity of what science really is, and what it has been trying to do ever since Galileo turned his telescope on the moons of Jupiter and invented the idea of believing what we see, instead of seeing what we believe.

His treatise, *Sidereus Nuncius*, which he wrote in 1610 to describe what he had seen, and from which this play takes its name, was composed in New Latin, the seventeenth-century language of scholars and churchmen. But Galileo wrote his later books in Italian, for anyone to read who could read. In them he reconceived the sky over our heads as a theater of the actual, something that belongs to everyone; which is all that any diligent plodder behind the scenes at a planetarium or a playhouse aspires to create here on Earth.

May 2019

The Starry Messenger received its world premiere, presented by The New Group (Scott Elliott, Artistic Director; Geoff Rich, Executive Director; Oliver Dow, Managing Director), at the Acorn Theatre, Theatre Row, New York City, on 23 November 2009, with the following cast:

MARK	Matthew Broderick
ANNE	J. Smith-Cameron
ANGELA	Catalina Sandino Moreno
ARNOLD	Grant Shaud
NORMAN	Merwin Goldsmith
DORIS	Missy Yager
MRS PYSNER	Stephanie Cannon
IAN/ADAM	Kieran Culkin

Director	Kenneth Lonergan
Set	Derek McLane
Costume	Mattie Ullrich
Lighting	Jason Lyons
Sound	Shane Rettig
Projections	Austin Switser

The Starry Messenger received its UK premiere, presented by Simon Friend Entertainment, at Wyndham's Theatre, London, on 29 May 2019 (previews from 16 May), with the following cast:

MARK	Matthew Broderick
ANNE	Elizabeth McGovern
ANGELA	Rosalind Eleazar
ARNOLD	Joplin Sibtain
NORMAN	Jim Norton
DORIS	Sinead Matthews
MRS PYSNER	Jenny Galloway
IAN/ADAM	Sid Sagar
Understudies	Edward Wolstenholme
	Helen Barford
	Kerry Bennett
	Greg Baxter
Director	Sam Yates
Designer	Chiara Stephenson
Lighting	Neil Austin
Sound and Music	Alex Baranowski
Projections	Luke Halls
Casting	Ginny Schiller CDG
Associate Director	Rebecca Hill

Characters

MARK WILLIAMS, *an astronomy teacher at the Hayden Planetarium, forties*
ANNE WILLIAMS, *his wife, an elementary school teacher, forties*
ANGELA VASQUEZ, *a secretary and trainee nurse, late twenties/early thirties*
ARNOLD STANTON, *Mark's colleague at the Planetarium, forties*
NORMAN KETTERLY, *a cancer patient, around seventy*
DORIS, *his daughter, forties*
IAN, *Mark's student, twenties*
MRS PYSNER, *Mark's student, forties–fifties*
ADAM, *Mark and Anne's son, fifteen – an offstage character played by the actor who plays Ian*

Setting

The play takes place in Manhattan and White Plains, New York.

Time

Fall 1996.

This text went to press before the end of rehearsals and so may differ slightly from the play as performed.

ACT ONE

Scene One

A classroom in the basement of the Hayden Planetarium in New York City, September of 1996.

A slide appears of the Earth, seen from space. MARK WILLIAMS *speaks in the semi-dark. He is in his forties. He has dressed with care for his class.*

MARK. This of course, is our own Earth. Rather distinctive. Very easy to recognize. (*Pointing.*) Here's my house. Here's the Planetarium...

The class laughs politely. Another slide: the Earth rising above the surface of the Moon.

And of course, the famous shot of the Earth rising above the lunar surface taken by the rather... *fortunate* Apollo astronauts. A much more imposing sight than our view the Moon, the Earth appears four times larger in the lunar sky than the Moon appears in ours...

MRS PYSNER, *one of the students, raises her hand.*

MRS PYSNER. Question? Question?

MARK. I hear a question from the dark. Yes?

MRS PYSNER. Yes – Yes – Now – Why is that? (*Pause*)

MARK. Why is...

MRS PYSNER. Why does the Earth appear larger than the Moon?

MARK. Well... Because the Earth is indeed... four times larger.

MRS PYSNER. But – I – Aren't they the same distance from each other?

MARK. Um, yes – Yes they are.

MRS PYSNER. So why don't they... I don't understand.

MARK (*not sure what problem is*). Well… since the Earth is larger than the Moon, and the distance between them is a relatively constant one, naturally the larger celestial body appears… larger.

MRS PYSNER (*unconvinced*). I see.

MARK. All right?

MRS PYSNER (*unconvinced*). Yeah…

A blank slide.

MARK. Just a moment…

He fiddles with the projector trigger.

If I can get this to… we'll move on to Mars, which is the next planet out from the Sun…

Another blank slide.

…lf we can find it…

A slide of a woman posing in front of a scenic view.

I beg your pardon. This is my wife. Not, of course, the planet Mars.

The class laughs.

Somehow seem to have gotten these… there we are.

A slide of Mars.

The planet Mars. The Red Planet. Ares, God of War:

MRS PYSNER. Question?

MARK. Yes.

MRS PYSNER. Now… Mars is a planet? Or a moon?

MARK. Mars is a planet, like our own Earth. Planets go around, or orbit, stars – such as our own Sun. Moons go around, or orbit, planets.

MRS PYSNER. And Mars… goes around…

MARK. The Sun.

There is a big laugh from the classroom next door to them.
IAN, a young man in his early twenties, raises his hand.

IAN. Professor Williams?

MARK. Yes.

IAN. Yeah, can I ask like what determined the actual *size* of the planets when the Solar System was being formed? I mean, what actually caused the differentiation between the sizes of the Earth and Mars and Jupiter. Was it just totally random? Or was there some kind of relationship between the elements the planets are made of and their eventual size?

MARK. Well, we can – we'll be getting to that, uh, later on, when we discuss the formation of the Solar System – But let's not get ahead of ourselves –

IAN. Oh, okay.

MARK. But it's an excellent question, and we'll – try to answer it – uh, when we get to that – uh – area.

IAN. Okay.

Another big laugh from next door.

MARK. Ah. That is our intermediate course, taught by my colleague Arnold Stanton, who has a rather *unique* teaching style. In any case, you will be hearing this periodically. Don't let it interfere with, uh...

Another big laugh.

...with your enjoyment of *my* hilarious remarks.

MARK*'s class laughs slightly.*

Some of you may be familiar with Arnold from his regular contributions to *Natural History* magazine, and *Astronomy* magazine, of course... In any case. Now: we have some rather spectacular photographs of the Martian surface, of the actual surface of Mars, courtesy of the Viking mission which as you may know set down an unmanned spacecraft on the surface of the red planet and took these rather incredible color photographs.

Slides of the Martian surface.

Isn't that wonderful?

He clicks through a few more of the Viking photos. The slide projector goes off, the lights go on.

Well, I see we are out of time for this week. I will see you all next week. We will be covering the fundamentals of astronomy – covering the basics of our present-day knowledge about the nature of our planet, our Solar System, the galaxy, the universe.

There's no homework required, of course. No exams, no surprise quizzes, no public humiliation –

The class laughs politely.

We assume you are here at the Planetarium for the pleasure of acquiring new knowledge. And we have a pretty good turnout this year, very gratifying… Um, sixteen of you in this section, I think… Um, let's see. Oh – it's eighteen, actually. In any case, I hope you find the course enjoyable. And I'll see you next week.

The students rise. MRS PYSNER *and* IAN *start gathering their belongings as* MARK *fusses with his slide projector.*

MRS PYSNER (*loud whisper*). I think he's kind of boring, don't you?

The students exit. MARK *stands there, having overheard this remark. He starts packing his slides.* ARNOLD STANTON, *forties, sticks his head in the door.*

ARNOLD. Hey. Want to get a beer?

MARK. Oh. No. Thanks, Arnold. Anne's expecting me.

ARNOLD. Okay. Good group?

MARK. Yes. They seem nice.

ARNOLD. Great. Great. Hey, I heard you got pretty close on that thing with Herschel.

MARK. Oh. Well. It was more of an exercise than anything else. But I certainly enjoyed making the rounds.

ARNOLD. You know who they hired?

MARK. I do. His name is, uh, Ben Rothberg. He was a grad student of mine, oh, fifteen years ago it must have been, back in New Haven…

ARNOLD. Yeah, no, I heard. I know Ben.

MARK. He's a very sharp guy. I think they made a good decision. I didn't actually expect to be seriously considered.

ARNOLD. Well, sure you don't want to grab a beer?

MARK. No thanks. I should really get home. Thursday.

ARNOLD. Okay. Hey, how's your mom holding up, okay?

MARK. She's fine…

ARNOLD. Yeah. God. I guess we're gettin' to that age.

MARK. Yes… I'm afraid so…

ARNOLD. All right. Give my best to Anne.

MARK. I'll see you later, Arnold.

> ARNOLD *goes out, past* ANGELA VASQUEZ, *who stands in the doorway now. She is in her late twenties/early thirties. She wears a raincoat over office clothes.*

> Yes. Hello?

ANGELA. Hi, I'm sorry. Is this the six-thirty astronomy class?

MARK. It was. Can I help you?

ANGELA. Yeah, is this where you sign up to take the course?

MARK. Um, no. No it's not. You have to call the Planetarium in the daytime and they'll give you all the information.

MARK. But if you like I'd be   ANGELA. But can I just ask –
    happy to –   I'm sorry:
That's all right.

ANGELA. Can I just ask, what level the class is at?

MARK. It's a very basic level.

ANGELA. Because –

MARK. It's a basic nuts-and-bolts Introduction to Astronomy. This class is. Um…

ANGELA. Do you think it's suitable for a nine-year-old? Probably not, right?

MARK. No... I wouldn't say so. It's a two and a half hour class. It's an adult class. For beginners. We do have –

ANGELA. They don't teach a class for children here?

MARK. Oh yes, there's a Saturday morning class – it's geared more toward kids. Although I believe they're more or less mid-cycle just now.

ANGELA. Oh, okay. Do you know when do they start up again?

MARK. That depends on the class. You can call the Planetarium during the day and they'll have all that information

ANGELA. Yeah, okay, I'm sorry –

MARK. No no – If you like, I can write down the number for you...

ANGELA. Oh thank you. My son is really interested in astronomy and the science program in his school is kind of weak? So I thought... Anyway, I'm sorry to bother you.

MARK. No bother.

ANGELA. Thank you. You know I live three blocks from here and I never came in before? It's really beautiful.

MARK. Oh, the Planetarium is wonderful. You should bring your son sometime.

ANGELA. Yeah, I would like to. I really like that big meteor they have upstairs.

MARK. You should take him to see one of the, uh, one of the Sky Shows.

ANGELA. Okay. (*Pause*) What's that?

MARK. Oh, well, it used to be... it used to be wonderful. There's a projection machine in the Sky Theater – the Zeiss 6. It's just extraordinary. It can do anything; it can project exact simulations of the stars on the, uh, on the big dome, from any time of the year, or any time in history, or any time in the future. (*A joke:*) Barring some universal cataclysm. But the whole Planetarium is wonderful. They're tearing it down, of course.

ANGELA. They are?

MARK. Yes, they're, um, tearing it down and building some hideous glass monstrosity in its place –

ANGELA. Oh that's too bad. I didn't know that. I really like it… It's so gloomy.

MARK. It's just old. The whole place is old.

ANGELA. No, I like the atmosphere. It's so quiet… It's really nice.

MARK. Well, there's no one in the building… Except the janitors. (*Pause*) Have you ever seen the, uh, the Christmas show?

ANGELA. No.

MARK. Oh. Well. They have a Christmas show they still do, about the Star of Bethlehem, that I used to come and see every year, as a kid. Every year my parents would take my sisters and me into the city to see the *Nutcracker* ballet –

ANGELA. 'My sisters and I.'

MARK. I'm sorry?

ANGELA. It's 'my sisters and I.' You said 'my sisters and me.'

MARK. Um – (*To himself.*) 'My sisters and…' (*To her.*) No, it is 'my sisters and me.' 'My sister and me' is correct.

ANGELA. It is? Oh all right. I guess it – God. All right. Duh!

MARK. Quite all right.

ANGELA. That's embarrassing!

MARK. No no – quite all right. In any case, my parents would take my sisters and me into the city to see the *Nutcracker* ballet and the Star of Bethlehem Sky Show. I remember driving as a kid, driving up and seeing the big green dome… (*Pause*) Am I boring you?

ANGELA. No.

MARK. In any case, the Christmas show is somewhat fanciful… But it's fun. (*Pause*)

ANGELA. What is it? Do they do like a –

MARK. Oh. Well, it's about the, uh, the Star of Bethlehem –

ANGELA. Oh yeah. Uh-huh?

MARK. And whether it had any basis in, um, astronomical fact.

ANGELA. Did it?

MARK. Oh probably not. It's all speculation. But my favorite part is the very end. When the announcer says something to the effect of, 'Was there a supernova in the heavens that night two thousand years ago? Was it a visiting comet? Or a unique alignment of the planets? Or was it something else? Science can only provide us with part of the answer. The rest is up to you.' And then they play this wonderful chord from the, um, from the end of Beethoven's 6th Symphony... And they project an image of the Star of Bethlehem shining down across the dome on the three wise men on their camels. Very silly... But I liked it.

ANGELA. Why is it silly?

MARK. Oh – I don't know... In any case. This'll be the last year they ever do it. Which is a shame... It's a very New York institution.

ANGELA. I'm definitely gonna bring David. I think he would really like it. (*Pause*)

MARK. In any case... I should be going home...

ANGELA. Okay. Me too.

MARK. And if you just call the Planetarium in the morning, they'll be able to give you all the program information for the year...

ANGELA. Okay, thanks. I will.

MARK. Oh, it's no problem. My name is Mark. By the way.

ANGELA. Hi, I'm Angela.

MARK. Nice to meet you, Angela.

They shake hands.

ANGELA. It was nice to meet you too. It's really nice talking to you.

MARK. It was very nice talking to you too.

ANGELA. Yeah...

MARK. Why don't you bring your son around sometime? I'll give you a backstage tour.

ANGELA. Really? That's so nice of you.

MARK. Oh, not at all, it's easily arranged. (*Pause*)

ANGELA. So what should I do? Like... just come by?

MARK. Oh. No – I'll give you my, uh, my office number. I'm here twice a week, six to nine. I teach at City College Monday through Friday, but late afternoons are good...

ANGELA. Okay. Thank you...!

MARK writes down and gives her his number.

MARK. Call any time.

ANGELA. Thanks a lot. Oh my God, it's so late. I'm sorry.

MARK. Oh, that's all right. Where is David now?

ANGELA. He's with my sister. But she only lives a few blocks away.

MARK. Oh so that's convenient.

ANGELA. Oh God, without her, forget it. My sisters, my mother... Do you have any kids?

MARK. Yes. One son.

ANGELA. Oh, just like me.

MARK. Mm-hm. Here, I'll walk out with you. Let me just get the, uh...

She goes to the door. He goes to the light switch.

ANGELA. Ready?

MARK. Yes, I'm ready.

He turns off the light.

Scene Two

Crossfade to MARK *and* ANNE*'s house in White Plains.* ANNE WILLIAMS, *forties, is going through some paperwork at the table.* MARK *enters. He is not happy to be home.*

MARK. Hello.

ANNE. Hi honey. How are you?

MARK. Okay.

ANNE. Did you get something to eat?

MARK. Yes.

ANNE. How was the class?

MARK. Good. Seems like a good group. Sixteen in tonight's section, eighteen in Thursday's section. Um – other way around. Sixteen on Thursday, eighteen on Tuesdays.

ANNE. That's a good turnout, isn't it?

MARK. Yes, very good.

ANNE. Is anything wrong?

MARK. No. I'm just a little tired.

ANNE. Yeah, you must be.

MARK. Are you going to have anything to drink?

ANNE. I had a glass of wine. Are you going to have something?

MARK. Maybe I'll have a Scotch.

ANNE. That's a good idea.

He doesn't move.

MARK. How was your day?

ANNE. Oh, great. The 4th grade has lice.

MARK. Oh no.

ANNE. But Carrie and I   MARK. Please not lice.
checked our kids – Well
now, wait a minute –

MARK. I'd honestly rather kill us all now than go through that again.

ANNE. Listen to me, Carrie and I checked out all our kids and we couldn't find anything. I got us the shampoo just in case. But that's all we did all day was check them for lice.

MARK. All right.

ANNE. Oh, and Mark, I talked to my mother: She and her friend Eleanor want to come in December, on the weekend of the 11th, and stay till that Tuesday.

MARK. Who's Eleanor?

ANNE. She's her neighbour? Her friend. Whose husband died last year. They met at that widows' group?

MARK. I don't remember.

ANNE. Yes you do. We had lunch with her and her son.

MARK. Oh, yes.

ANNE. Anyway, she wants to bring Eleanor because Eleanor's never been to New York before, and they want to stay for three or four days and I told her it was all right but I wanted to ask you...

MARK. I don't mind. It's fine.

ANNE. I thought you might not want Eleanor.

MARK. I don't particularly. But that's all right. I want you to feel free to invite your mother...

ANNE. Yeah, and she'll have a much better time.

MARK. It's fine.

ANNE. Okay. I'll tell them to come.

MARK. Fine. *Which* weekend?

ANNE. December 11th? I figured we could either put them both in the spare room or if they don't want to sleep in the same room one of them could sleep on the pullout sofa.

MARK. Okay.

ANNE. It'd probably be better for Mom to have the bedroom because she likes to have her own bathroom.

MARK. Mm.

ANNE. But I'm gonna leave that up to her. Or we could help them figure out a hotel, or a hotel for Eleanor. But I think they'll probably want to both stay here. You know, they probably want to go into the city and see a show – that kind of thing. They wanted to know what shows were good. They probably want to see a musical. I thought maybe one night we could all drive into the city and have dinner and see a show and that way...

MARK. Okay...

ANNE. That way we'll know we really did something with them...

MARK. That seems like a good plan.

ANNE. Do you know what shows are supposed to be good now? I don't even know what's playing.

MARK. I don't really. I don't either.

ANNE. They'll probably just want to see a big Broadway musical. They're not the most sophisticated audience in the world... We could just take them to *Les Miz*. Or something. *Phantom of the Opera*.

MARK. Okay.

ANNE. Do you think we should have dinner too? Dinner and show?

MARK. Sure. That sounds good.

ANNE. Okay. Where do you think we should eat?

MARK. I don't know. That place Charlie's was good. But anything's fine – honestly.

ANNE. Oh. I didn't like that place so much.

MARK. Then let's go somewhere else. We don't have to decide tonight.

ANNE. All right... Do you want me to fix you a drink?

MARK. I'll make it.

MARK *gets up and starts mixing a drink.*

Do you want one?

ANNE. No thanks. Can we talk about Christmas for a minute?

MARK. Yes.

ANNE. My sister wants to have it at her house. But I told her your
mother invited us to go up there. So I said I would ask you.
I also thought we could bring your mother with us if we did go
to my sister's.

MARK. What do you want to do?

ANNE. I don't know. I wanted to get your opinion about it. If we
don't go to your mother's we might have to drive out there and
get her – Or we could have her come over a day or two before
and then all go to Jody's on Christmas. Or we could do
something here on Christmas Eve and have that be our
Christmas, and then all go out to Jody's on Christmas Day. But
since my mother's coming now, with Eleanor, two weekends
before Christmas, I thought you might not want to do all that so
close together.

MARK. It's too complicated. I don't know.

ANNE. It's *not* complicated. I just want to know if you want to go
out to my sister's on Christmas instead of having people here, or
if that's too much of an ordeal because your mother can't drive
herself, and we would have to go get her and have her here an
extra day or two.

MARK. I don't understand what the choices are. I don't care.
(*Pause*)

ANNE. Are you mad at me about something? Or are you just upset
about Herschel?

MARK. Neither. I'm not mad, and I'm not especially upset about
Herschel. As a matter of fact, I was encouraged that it went as
far as it did. I'm just a little irritable. I don't mean to take it out
on you.

ANNE. It's just that you never want to talk about it, but when
I make the arrangements myself you don't like that either. So it's
a little unfair.

MARK. Honestly Anne, anything is fine. I just can't talk about it right now. Whatever you said is fine. I can't – think. I don't know. I – possibly didn't get enough sleep and I can't concentrate. I'm not trying to be unhelpful.

ANNE. But when *do* you want to talk about Christmas?

MARK. Tomorrow.

ANNE. When?

MARK. Five o'clock.

ANNE. I don't get home till six…

MARK. I'll be proud to talk about Christmas at six-fifteen.

ANNE. Thank you.

MARK. You're welcome. Where is Adam?

ANNE. In the basement.

MARK *takes his drink, goes to the basement door and opens it.*

MARK. Hi Adam.

ADAM (*off*). Hey Dad.

MARK. How are you?

ADAM (*off*). Fine. (*Pause*)

MARK. Would you like to know how I am?

ADAM (*off*). How are you, Dad?

MARK. I'm fine.

ADAM (*off*). That is really good news.

MARK. Thank you for asking.

ADAM (*off*). It was no problem at all.

MARK. I'm glad we could have this chance to talk.

ADAM (*off*). I enjoyed the entire conversation.

MARK *closes the door.*

MARK. He and I are developing a real bond.

ANNE. Don't be so hard on him. He's fifteen.

MARK. I know he's fifteen. I'm not being hard on him.

He sits on the sofa and turns on the TV. A sitcom comes on.

SITCOM ACTOR. Could we get back to the subject of Marcie's butt for a second?

Canned laughter. MARK *changes the channels.*

NEWS ANNOUNCER. – discovery of mass graves outside the Croatian village by UN Peacekeepers –

MARK. Oh good.

NEWS ANNOUNCER. – who said the bodies of at least seventeen men and boys appeared to have been buried there as recently as six months earlier…

NEWS ANNOUNCER.
…A spokesman for the UN said that that many of the bodies appear to have to been badly mutilated. The village is one of several in the area occupied by Serb forces last year. Witnesses describe Serbian troops evacuating the female population in buses, raising additional fears fueled by continuing reports of mass rapes –

ANNE. Could we possibly watch something else?

MARK. Don't you want to hear about mass graves?

ANNE. Not at the moment, no.

MARK *starts changing channels.*

MARK. When I was fifteen I was interested in things.

ANNE. He's interested in things. He's interested in everything.

MARK *flips channels.* ANNE *goes back to her school papers.*

Scene Three

Crossfade to a private room in Sloan Kettering Hospital. ANGELA
comes in wearing nurse's trainee scrubs. The patient is NORMAN
KETTERLY, *around seventy. He's very ill. Right now he's feeling so
sick he can barely speak for fear of throwing up.* (*Note:* ANGELA
can also walk NORMAN *in slowly and carefully under the crossfade,
and help him in or out of bed before the crossfade is complete.*)

ANGELA. How are you doing, Norman?

NORMAN. Not so good.

ANGELA. Are you in pain?

NORMAN. I don't know.

ANGELA. What's bothering you?

NORMAN. I don't know. Everything. I don't feel so hot.

ANGELA. You want me to get one of the nurses?

NORMAN. What do you mean? What are you?

ANGELA. I'm not on duty. I was just on the floor so I wanted to
come see how you were doing.

NORMAN. Oh – Thank you. Not so great.

ANGELA. But do you want me to get somebody for you?

NORMAN. I wouldn't know what to tell them. Don't ask me that
anymore. I just don't feel good.

ANGELA. Okay. I'll just let you try to sleep…

NORMAN. Don't go. Just sit down a minute. I just don't want to
take a quiz right now. I just can't answer anything.

ANGELA. Sure. Okay. I understand.

She sits down next to his bed. His eyes are closed.

You know you may be feeling bad because they changed your
medication. It may be giving you some nausea.

NORMAN. I don't know.

ANGELA. When the doctor comes you should try to tell him
what's the matter and maybe they can adjust your medication.

NORMAN. Yes. Thanks. I will. Thank you.

ANGELA. What time is Doris coming?

NORMAN. I don't know. What time is it now?

ANGELA. A little before eight.

NORMAN. At night?

ANGELA. Yeah.

NORMAN. If it's going to be like this I'd just as soon get out of it. You know?

ANGELA. I know.

NORMAN. I mean I'd like to get better, but I can't go through much more of this. I mean it. My kids are grown up. I did my best. I don't want to be a quitter, but what am I doing it for?

ANGELA. I know.

NORMAN. Maybe I could try a little ginger ale.

ANGELA. Sure, okay.

She goes to the fridge and gets out a ginger ale. Opens it.

You want some ice with that?

NORMAN. No thanks. I don't need a cup.

She brings it to him. He sips it.

ANGELA. Not too fast.

NORMAN. That's really good.

ANGELA. Just take little sips.

NORMAN. That's delicious.

ANGELA. I think you're feeling a little better.

NORMAN. I think so. Thank you. That's enough. Thank you.

ANGELA. I'll just put it right here.

NORMAN. Okay. Thank you. Thank you.

She puts the ginger ale next to his bed.

How is your mother?

ANGELA. She's all right.

NORMAN. How's her neck?

ANGELA. Oh it's a lot better. Thanks for asking. I'm trying to get her to go to a massage therapist but she's so stubborn she won't go.

NORMAN. How's your shit husband?

ANGELA. He's not a shit. He's just got a lot of problems.

NORMAN. He's a piece of shit.

ANGELA. No he's not. Don't say that!

NORMAN. I don't care.

ANGELA. He's just a baby. I don't care how he is with me. I don't like the way he is with David.

NORMAN. Why? How is he?

ANGELA. Oh he's always just like, he doesn't really take an interest but he always wants David to respect him, then all of a sudden he turns around and acts like he's all strict and he's gonna show me the right way to bring him up.

NORMAN. A shit.

ANGELA. I guess he's sort of shitty, but I don't like to be saying that about him to everybody in case we ever get back together again.

NORMAN. It's very unlikely that he and I will ever meet.

ANGELA. They said you had a lot of visitors today…

NORMAN. My stepson came by with his wife.

ANGELA. Do you get along with them?

NORMAN. They're all right. They're pretty dumb. I wish the hell she would get here so I could go to sleep.

ANGELA. Go to sleep. I don't want to keep you up.

NORMAN. Don't go yet, will you? It makes a big difference having some company. Besides you smell very nice. You don't smell like urine.

He pats her hand and then holds on to it.

ANGELA. Thank you, Norman. That's really flattering.

NORMAN. I would never say it if it wasn't true. Go home if you want to. I don't want to keep you.

ANGELA. I could stay a minute.

NORMAN. Thank you. I'm just gonna close my eyes for a minute.

ANGELA. That's all right.

NORMAN. Thank you, sweetheart.

ANGELA. You're welcome.

> NORMAN *closes his eyes.* ANGELA *stays by his bedside, still holding his hand. She checks her watch, decides she has a few minutes, then reaches awkwardly to pick up a magazine with her free hand, opens it and starts reading.*

Scene Four

Crossfade to MARK*'s classroom. A slide of a spiral galaxy appears.* MARK *speaks to the class.*

MARK. Tonight we will be examining our own galaxy, the Milky Way. Now, here in the city, even on the clearest of nights, you can't really see the faintly luminous band that stretches across the night sky – because of course, the bright lights of the city blot it out. But remove yourself from the blazing city lights, and on any moonless night, look up and you will see the broad, winding, hazy band of luminosity which we call the Milky Way. Now. What is it we are actually looking at? Well. Imagine if you will a great, thick pinwheel, much like this one, comprised of stars and gas and dust. Our own little Solar System can be found somewhere near the edge – in the suburbs, as it were. Turn that wheel on its edge, and there you have our view. We are looking from near the rim, into the wheel –

> MRS PYSNER *has raised her hand.*

MRS PYSNER. Question? Question?

MARK. Yes?

MRS PYSNER. Okay – But – We're not actually *inside* it, right?

MARK. Yes. We are. And if –

MRS PYSNER. Okay, wait a minute, we're inside it?

MARK. Yes – We're part of –   IAN (*to* MRS PYSNER).
The Milky Way is a galaxy: Yeah, we're inside the
Our galaxy: wheel, see?

MRS PYSNER. Yes, I understand that part.

MARK. And our Solar System   MRS PYSNER. I guess I don't
is located – Well, just a –   understand where the wheel is.
Hold on. Hold on. These are
good questions –

IAN (*to* MRS PYSNER). And our planets go around the middle of *that*. (*Pause*)

MARK. No.

IAN. No: I mean, our *stars* go around the middle of that.

MARK. Yes. That's right. Exactly right. Yes.

MRS PYSNER. Then where do –

IAN (*simultaneous*). So can I ask like what exactly caused the *formation* of the various galaxies? I mean why did they disperse themselves into these various pinwheel shapes, or nebula shapes, or what have you? Was that just totally random, or is there some gravitational *law*…? I mean, is that just how it went after the Big Bang? I mean, like, why pinwheels? Or is that like a really dumb question?

MARK. No. No no. None of these questions are dumb –

MRS PYSNER. I'm sorry: I still don't understand where the wheel is. We're going around… the Sun. And our Sun is a star. And our star… is what.

MARK. Part of the –   IAN. Part of the Milky Way.
Yes. Exactly.

MRS PYSNER. Well I can't visualize it.

MARK. All right:

IAN (*simultaneous, to* MRS PYSNER). Just think of it in units. Like our planet is like a house, and our house is on a street, and that street is in a town, and the town is on an island – I'm sorry. I'm talking way too much.

MARK. Not at all:

MRS PYSNER. What do you mean, an island?

MARK. ...however, let me reclaim the floor here. (*To* IAN.) Now, you had a question about the formation of the galaxies...

IAN. Yeah.

MARK. Okay, *hold* that. Let me answer that in due course. Because I'd like to stick to our own galaxy for a moment...

IAN. Sure.

MARK *projects a slide of a spiral galaxy.*

MARK. Which, if we could get a shot from this angle, would look quite a bit like this one. This is a galaxy called NGC 2997. A beautiful spiral-armed galaxy very much like our own – Hello? Hello? If you wouldn't mind – I'm sorry. It's just too difficult –

IAN (*to* MRS PYSNER). See, if you break it down in units: like the Earth is a house, the Solar System's like a town, the galaxy is like a country, and the universe is like, a continent – (*To* MARK.) I'm sorry. I know. I'm really sorry.

Pause.

MARK. In any case, this is not our galaxy. It's a galaxy very similar to ours. Hello?

IAN (*whispers*). But that's a good mnemonic to keep it in your head. (*To* MARK.) I'm really sorry.

MRS PYSNER. I thought you said our galaxy was shaped like the side of a pinwheel.

MARK. No – It's –

MRS PYSNER (*reads from her notes*). 'The galaxy is shaped like the side of a pinwheel.'

MARK. Yes...

MRS PYSNER. I didn't make that *up*…

MARK.…but only if you're looking at it from the *side*.

MRS PYSNER. *What?*

MARK. Which of course, we are.

MRS PYSNER. I don't understand.

MARK. I'm saying that we're looking at it from our perspective.

IAN. We're looking at *that*, from the side. We're looking at it from our side of the galaxy.

MRS PYSNER. What…?

MARK. Okay. It's okay.

MARK *switches between the two slides to illustrate his point.*

Look: *This* is what our galaxy looks like. We are *here*, inside it, looking *this* way, and what we see is *this*. (*Pause*)

MRS PYSNER. Right. Okay.

MARK (*to* IAN). Now, as to *your* question about the formation of the galaxies – No, we let no question pass untouched-on here –

IAN. Oh, no, that's okay. Really it's okay.

IAN (*starts to rise*). Um, yeah, but, uh, I actually have to go.

MARK. Oh. Well, we can always –

IAN (*sits again*). But go ahead. I just – I have to leave in like five minutes.

MRS PYSNER. I have a question.

MARK. Yes?

MRS PYSNER. How do you know what it looks like at all?

MARK. Well, that we know from –

MRS PYSNER. I mean how do we know any of this?

MARK. Well, that's actually a perf–

MRS PYSNER. How do we even know the Earth is really round?

MARK. All right:

MRS PYSNER. I mean, unless it's *not*. Because it sure looks flat to me. Anyway, isn't it all pretty much just a theory?

MARK. No, it's round.

MRS PYSNER. But how do we *know*?

MARK. Well:

There is a big laugh from next door.

MRS PYSNER (*shrewdly*). But do you see what I mean?

MARK. Yes, I do see what you mean, and I'd like to…	MRS PYSNER. Do you see what I mean? I'm sorry. Go ahead.

MARK. All right: There are easily a dozen experiments you could do to prove that the Earth is round. But the real reason most of us know the Earth is round is because somebody found out before us, and *told* us so. However, let's suppose that I have a theory that there is a force – Gravity – that will pull me to the ground if there is nothing in the way.

He climbs up on the desk.

I will now do an experiment to test my theory. Watching? Okay. Here goes.

He jumps off the desk.

And *now* I *know* there is a force that will pull me toward the ground. I don't know why, I don't know how, I don't know much, but I can do the same experiment again and again and get the exact same result; it is not a theory and it's not an opinion. Now maybe this is all a dream I'm having, but I guarantee you that in this *particular* dream, every time somebody jumps off a chair, dives into a swimming pool, or gets pushed out a window, anywhere on this planet, I guarantee you he is going to fall toward the ground at the rate of ten meters per second squared. There are similar experiments you can do to prove to yourself that the Earth is round, if you care to do so. Such as flying into outer space and *looking* at it. Although that is a fairly recent option. Now, we certainly don't know everything, and it's quite possible we never will. But that doesn't mean the Earth is flat.

To say so is to say that the sky is green. You can say it all you like, but it's just not so. Whatever *round* is, so is the Earth. And that's all the time we have left for today.

IAN (*writing in his notebook*). Mm. Yes.

The students leave. IAN exits. MRS PYSNER approaches MARK.

MARK. Hi. Hi. I hope that was at least partially helpful.

MRS PYSNER. Yeah: I wanna say something here.

MARK. All righty. Shoot.

She waits for the remaining students to leave.

MARK. Was there something you –   MRS PYSNER. Yeah: I don't appreciate the sarcasm…!

MARK. I'm sorry?

MRS PYSNER. I don't appreciate the sarcasm! I'm trying –

MARK. I wasn't being sarcastic…!

MRS PYSNER. I'm sorry. I'm sorry. But yes you were. Yes you were.

MARK. I was really not being –   MRS PYSNER. I am trying *so hard* to understand this material, and I really don't appreciate being made fun of when I can't understand something right away.

MARK. I really did not mean or ever intend to make fun of you, or to seem like I was trying to be sarcastic in any way. If I was emphatic, or if I was trying to make a point –

MRS PYSNER. Then what is with the Fred Astaire routine?

MARK. I'm sorry?

MRS PYSNER. What was with the Flyin' Dutchman act?

MARK. Oh you mean – because I was – when I jumped off the desk?

MRS PYSNER. You know what I'm talkin' about.

MARK. If you're talking about my demonstration… of gravity –

MRS PYSNER. Demonstration my foot!

MARK. Ma'am, it *was* a   MRS PYSNER. If that's a
demonstration. It was meant   demonstration, I'm a
to be dramatic –   monkey's uncle.

MARK. – meant to make an impact. But that was a genuine
demonstration of the force of gravity in action.

MRS PYSNER. But how does jumping off a desk demonstrate the
force of *gravity*?

MARK. Because I fell down. Because – It demonst– Because
gravity is the force which pulls us toward the Earth.

MRS PYSNER. But not when you fall *down*.

MARK. Yes. Falling down is gravity pulling you toward the earth.

MRS PYSNER. But then why don't you go faster?

MARK. Faster than what? (*Pause*) You do go faster. Depending –

MRS PYSNER. So when they say the force of gravity, they mean
when it goes *down*?

MARK. Yes:

MARK. You had asked –   MRS PYSNER. But why don't
No: Excuse me. Excuse me.   you –
You had asked 'Isn't it all
pretty much a theory.' And
I was trying to demonstrate
in a dramatic way that you
can *prove* that there is such
a force as gravity and that   Well, now we're just goin'
it's not just –   around in circles.

MARK. Yes, because I want to convince you of what I'm saying.

MRS PYSNER (*near tears*). I don't understand why I'm having so
much trouble!

MARK. Neither do I. But first I would very much like you to
believe that I was really not making fun of you in any way –

MRS PYSNER. Yes, okay, I take it back!

MARK. You don't have to take it back if you don't –

MRS PYSNER. All right, I *don't* take it back. What do you want me to say? (*Pause*)

MARK. Well, I'm very sorry if I upset you. I will certainly try not to upset you again. I'm extremely sorry you've been so frustrated, and I take full responsibility for that. If you would like to meet for a few minutes before class to go over the material, I'm here at six o'clock every Tuesday and Thursday...

MRS PYSNER. I couldn't possibly be here by six.

MARK. Okay, well I'm sure we could work something out. And I appreciate your speaking up.

MRS PYSNER (*not at all mollified*). Yeah.

MARK. And I hope you have a good night.

MRS PYSNER. Mm-hm!

She exits. MARK *starts putting away his class materials.* ARNOLD *enters.*

ARNOLD. Hey buddy... Want to get a beer?

MARK. Yes I would.

ARNOLD. Great. Great. Listen, I'm having a problem with something in my section. Same problem every class. I've never been able to figure it out. I wonder if you could give me a little advice.

MARK. Sure, Arnold, what's the problem?

ARNOLD. Well, I've just always had a lot of trouble figuring out a really effective way to demonstrate the force of gravity. You know? Like just a simple, effective, dramatic demonstration.

MARK. That's very funny, Arnold.

ARNOLD. Like do you throw something in the *air*? Do you jump up and *down*? What do you do?

MARK. You know what, Arnold? The woman is trying to learn. She's trying to learn and she's frustrated. That's my fault. So let's uh, let's drop it. All right?

ARNOLD. Hey. Don't get mad at me.

MARK. I'm not mad at you. I know some of them are a bit eccentric.

ARNOLD. Eccentric?

MARK. But most of them are intelligent, interested people who are trying to learn something about our field. I do not see what's wrong with that.

ARNOLD. Neither do I, Mark, but that woman seems deranged.

MARK. Maybe she is. I don't know. Am I supposed to not try? I don't like it either...!

ARNOLD. What are you getting so mad about?

MARK. Come on, Arnold.

Pause.

ARNOLD. 'Come on Arnold' what?   MARK. This is just fun for you.

ARNOLD. What?

MARK. I said this is just fun for you. It'sssssss...

ARNOLD. What do you mean it's just fun for me?

MARK. It's all right. But you have a lot of irons in the fire...

ARNOLD. A lot of what?

MARK. It's – Come on. (*Pause*)

ARNOLD. You mean professionally?

MARK. Yes. It's – Yes. So it's slightly less funny to me. That's all.

ARNOLD. That's not why I think it's funny.

MARK. All right.

ARNOLD. Because I have other irons in the fire. (*Pause*) Anyway, you keep up. You know a lot of people. You got pretty close on that Moritz thing...

MARK. Come on, Arnold. The only reason I got as far as I did is because Herschel liked me when I was a kid. It was fun making the rounds, but it's obviously a waste of time to try to regain a toehold in a field where you've basically – gone as far as you're going to go. I have no complaints. I'm not doing so badly.

ARNOLD. You know there's another slot opening up?

MARK. What do you mean? What kind of slot?

ARNOLD. Apparently there's another slot, like a research assistant, or data analyst, or –

MARK. Oh?

ARNOLD. They may just be looking for a grad student, but it's with the project, so I thought you might be interested.

MARK. Oh no, I'll ask about it. Thank you.

ARNOLD. Can we get a beer now? I would like to drink some beer.

MARK. All right. Sure.

MARK *starts to gather up his stuff.*

ARNOLD. Hey, who was that girl you were showing around last week?

MARK. Oh – That was a, uh, a young woman – That was a woman.

ARNOLD. I saw she was a woman.

MARK. And her son – She wants to enroll her son in the kiddie class. I was supposed to give them a backstage tour.

ARNOLD. Where was the son?

MARK. Oh. He, uh, he couldn't do it at last minute. He got a sore throat or something. And she was nice enough… She didn't have a number to call to cancel so she came by. Very nice girl.

ARNOLD. All right. Just curious. It just seemed to me like your hair was very much nicer than usual.

MARK. Yes, I combed it.

ARNOLD. Should we get out of here?

MARK. Yes. I enjoyed your paper, by the way, Arnold. Very much.

ARNOLD. Oh. Thanks, Mark. We'll see how it goes over.

They go out.

Scene Five

Crossfade to NORMAN*'s hospital room.* ANGELA *is straightening up.* NORMAN*'s daughter* DORIS, *forties, comes in. She's got a bag full of supplies for him. Food and magazines, etc.*

DORIS. Oh hi, Angela. How are you?

ANGELA. Hi Doris. I'm fine thanks. How are you?

DORIS. I'm okay. How long has he been sleeping?

ANGELA. He just fell asleep. I just came in to say hello.

DORIS *puts some gourmet food items in the mini-fridge.*

DORIS. Who is on tonight?

ANGELA. Rowena and Denise?

DORIS. Uh-huh?

ANGELA. Do you want me to get them?

DORIS. No, I was just wondering. Do you know if Dr Kellogg is around?

ANGELA. I saw him before. You want me to go look for him?

DORIS. I'll find him in a minute… It seems very cold in here.

ANGELA. I know. They keep it so cold. We could put another blanket on him.

DORIS. Maybe we should.

ANGELA *feels* NORMAN*'s hand.*

ANGELA. He doesn't feel cold to me.

DORIS. Well let's leave it. How's your little boy?

ANGELA. He's good. Except he's really mad at me.

DORIS. Why?

ANGELA. 'Cause he started wearing glasses? And he hates them. And he looks so cute, you know? But it's probably more this schedule I'm on. It's really hard. It's only for a few more months, but that's a long time for a little kid.

DORIS. How old is he?

ANGELA. He's gonna be ten in January.

DORIS. Where is he tonight?

ANGELA. With my sister.

DORIS. Your sister takes care of him when you're working?

ANGELA. My sisters, my mother. Everybody helps out…
Everybody wants me to make it.

DORIS. Well, I think you're already terrific. You have a terrific
bedside manner.

ANGELA. It's easy with your father.

DORIS. It's easy for *you*.

ANGELA. He's just not afraid to be himself. He doesn't put up
with any BS.

DORIS. That's for sure. He doesn't put up with anything period.

ANGELA. You want to be alone with him?

DORIS. What for?

Pause.

ANGELA. Just… You know.

DORIS *looks like she's about to cry.*

It could really turn around you know.

DORIS. I know. I just wish it would go one way or the other.

ANGELA. I know, Doris, but it's really true. He has a good chance.
He is very strong:

DORIS. Yeah. So was my mother. Everybody on this ward is very
strong. The lady with the zippers on her skull is probably very
strong. She's gotta weigh seventy-eight pounds. I don't know
why her family doesn't kill her. What is she doing here? You
think my mother wasn't strong? You should have seen what they
put her through!

ANGELA. I know. But there's a lot more they can do now. And
they're not gonna lie to you. He could turn around tomorrow.

DORIS. I can't even get my sister to get on a fucking plane…!

ANGELA. I know. It's probably she's just scared, you know?

DORIS. You don't think I'm scared? I've been here every day for a month and a half!

ANGELA. I know. Some people just can't handle it –

DORIS. Just don't defend her, all right? I mean I appreciate it, but… I just don't understand her.

She gets ahold of herself.

ANGELA. You want some Kleenex?

DORIS. No, I have some, thank you. I'll be all right in a minute. (*Blows her nose, wipes her eyes.*) If you have to go home don't let me keep you. I'm all right.

ANGELA. All right… I'll see you on the weekend. I'm trailing Maureen, so I'll be on the floor from twelve to ten, Saturday and Sunday.

DORIS. And then you go to an office nine to five on Monday?

ANGELA. It's only for a few more months.

DORIS. Gee. All right. Well, good for you.

ANGELA. I'll see you on Saturday.

DORIS. Goodnight.

ANGELA *leaves.* DORIS *goes to* NORMAN. *Pause. Very tentatively, she leans over and tries to kiss him on the head. Before she can, he wakes up. She starts, and quickly steps back.*

NORMAN. Hey.

DORIS. Hi Dad.

NORMAN. What's the matter?

DORIS. Nothing. You were sleeping.

NORMAN. I guess I fell asleep.

ANGELA *comes back.*

ANGELA. Doris. Dr Kellogg is at the nurse's station if you want to talk to him.

DORIS. Oh. Thank you. I'll be right back.

She exits.

NORMAN. Could I have something to drink?

ANGELA. Sure, you want some ginger ale?

NORMAN. All right yeah.

She goes to the refrigerator.

I like your ass.

ANGELA. Thanks Norman, I like yours too.

NORMAN. Everybody likes my ass. It's natural to be envious...
How's your love life these days?

ANGELA. That's none of your business, Norman. Why? How's
yours?

NORMAN. It's been a challenge.

ANGELA. I'll tell you what. When you get better we'll go out,
okay?

NORMAN. Sorry, no, it wouldn't work, you're not my type.

ANGELA. Oh yeah? Why not? What's your type?

NORMAN. Oh, I like a predatory, unpleasant abusive kind of
woman who looks furious at me all the time and yells at me on
a kind of quota system. You wouldn't really fit into my lifestyle.

ANGELA. Oh, okay. Here. See if you can drink this.

She gives him some ginger ale.

I should really go home now.

NORMAN. I'll see you in the morning.

ANGELA. I'm not gonna be here in the morning, I'm only here on
weekends, ten to twelve, and then –

NORMAN. Okay, okay. It's not very interesting to hear about your
schedule all the time.

He looks at her.

You're such a pretty girl.

ANGELA. It's just the uniform.

NORMAN. Give me a kiss, will you?

> ANGELA *hesitates, then kisses* NORMAN. DORIS *comes in just in time to see this. They don't see her. She steps back.*

> Thank you.

ANGELA. I gotta go.

> *Going to the door, she sees* DORIS, *who pretends she's just coming in.*

> Goodnight, Doris.

DORIS. Goodnight.

Scene Six

Crossfade to ANGELA*'s apartment.* MARK *waits on the sofa.* ANGELA *comes in from the other room.*

ANGELA. He's asleep. Oh my God, he was so tired…

MARK. He's a very nice kid.

ANGELA. Ohh, thank you, Mark. That's so sweet of you. He had such a good time today. Thank you.

MARK. Oh – It was my pleasure. (*Pause*) I really like those glasses.

ANGELA. Oh my God, he hates them so much.

MARK. He'll get used to them.

ANGELA. You want a beer or some wine or something?

MARK. I would have a beer.

ANGELA. Is Lite Beer okay? I bought it by mistake. It's kind of gross.

MARK. Oh, anything's fine…

ANGELA. Do you want a glass – ?

MARK. No. Thank you. I shouldn't stay too long…

ANGELA. You could still have a glass.

MARK. That's all right, thanks.

She goes out. He waits. She comes back with a glass of beer.

Thank you. Aren't you going to have anything?

ANGELA. No…

She sits down on the other end of the sofa.

Thanks for being so nice to David.

MARK. Oh. That's all right. Entirely my pleasure…

ANGELA. Oh my God. He had such a good time.

MARK. Good. Always glad to enlist a new recruit…

ANGELA. Yeah…

MARK. He's just about the same age I was when I got interested in science, actually. Maybe a year or two older.

ANGELA. Oh yeah?

MARK. Mm-hm. Yeah.

ANGELA. Did you grow up in the city? In New York?

MARK. No. I'm from Connecticut originally. From right outside New Haven, originally. My mother still lives there. My father passed away recently…

ANGELA. Ohhh, I'm sorry.

MARK. Thank you. Are both your parents living?

ANGELA. Oh yeah. My mom lives a few blocks away, on 84th street. And my dad's in Puerto Rico.

MARK. Oh, do you get down there a lot?

ANGELA. Not really. I don't really see him very much. I used to go a lot when my grandmother was still alive, but… I don't really get along with him.

MARK. Mm-hm? And you told me you worked for the government, Angela…?

ANGELA. Yeah, I work for the Department of Fishing and Wildlife…?

MARK. That's right, that's right.

ANGELA. …I'm a secretary. In the Office of External Programs? That's like the Public Relations office?

MARK. Mm-hm?

ANGELA. Yeah. I'm also – I do all the FOIA (*Pronounced 'foya'.*) stuff, like I process the FOIA requests.

MARK. I don't know what that is.

ANGELA. That's the Freedom of Information Act? We call it FOIA…

MARK. Oh I see.

ANGELA. Yeah, they just made me the FOIA officer this year.

MARK. Oh, congratulations.

ANGELA. No, it's not like it's really a promotion. It's just like a different kind of paperwork. But it sounds kind of good to say it. You know, like to say I'm the FOIA officer and not just the secretary. It's a nice office, everybody's really nice…

MARK. Well that's always important.

ANGELA. I was gonna leave like three times: Like once I got another job offer that paid more, so I told them I had to quit, and everybody was really sad and they had this party for me, and then it turned out my boss got me this raise she thought she couldn't get me, so I decided to stay. But the next year I had to leave because I started working there in this government work program for kids – and you can't be employed under that unless you're under twenty-one, and I started right when I was eighteen. So that was gonna be my last year, right?

MARK. Uh-huh?

ANGELA. So they had another party for me and everybody got me presents, and they had a cake and wine and everything, and everybody signed a card and they made speeches and you know, like jokes about my personality, and how much they were gonna miss me. And then two days later my boss called me and told me she got the personnel department to hire me as a permanent employee, so I was back at work the next day, and everybody was laughing at me because they say like I just pretend to quit every year so I could get presents or something. It was really funny.

MARK. Your boss must like you.

ANGELA. I guess so. I'm very popular. No, I'm just kidding.

MARK. I'm sure you are...

ANGELA. But I'm in school to be a nurse now? So –

MARK. Oh really? I didn't realize.

ANGELA. Yeah, I have about six more months to go –

MARK. Well. That's very industrious.

ANGELA. Yeah, it's a lot, because it's two classes at night during the week, and then it's two ten-hour shifts on the weekend. But I'm really excited. Like, I can't believe it's really happening. But it's hard for David, but he knows it's only for a few more months.

MARK. Well, I think that's wonderful.

ANGELA. Thank you. (*Pause*) So do you like being a teacher?

MARK. Yes, for the most part. Yes. It's a bit... I don't know how much they really absorb... Or how much it really means to them. I started out with a – I started out trying to be a real astronomer. A practicing astronomer. (*Pause*) It's a long story...

ANGELA. That's all right.

MARK. Well... it's a very competitive field.

ANGELA. I bet you're a really good teacher.

MARK. Well, I'm a very experienced teacher anyway. (*Pause*) Where is David's father?

ANGELA. He's in Philadelphia.

MARK. How long has he been there?

ANGELA. Since last year.

MARK. What does he do there?

ANGELA. He's training to be an electrician. He's got a lot of problems. He's very unreliable with David.

MARK. That's too bad. I'm sorry to hear that.

ANGELA. Yeah... So what's your son like?

MARK. Oh... He's nice. A little rambunctious. He plays the guitar. Electric guitar. He's in a band.

ANGELA. What's it called?

MARK. Face the Muzak.

ANGELA. Face the Muzak. That's so cute. That's really good.

MARK. Yes, I think so too. You should hear the music. (*i.e. it's not very good.*)

ANGELA. Yeah, but that's all right. It's good he has different interests...

MARK. Oh absolutely. Absolutely. (*Pause*)

ANGELA. So... is this like... Never mind.

MARK. What?

ANGELA. Never mind. You'd probably think I'm really dumb.

MARK. Why would I?

ANGELA. Well, I don't know... Why do you have to be married? You're such a nice guy.

MARK. I'm sorry.

ANGELA. No, I don't mean like, 'Why are you married?' I just like talking to you. You're such a good listener. And you were so nice to David. I couldn't believe that. Like the way you explained everything to him. I don't know. Maybe you think it was weird I asked you to come up.

MARK. Not at all.

ANGELA. Maybe it is. Like maybe it's really weird that you're up here.

MARK. I don't think so.

ANGELA. That's all right: We could say it. We're not gonna *do* anything... But I mean... I don't know... The last two years have been really hard. There's a lot of support, but it's been really hard...

MARK *interrupts her to kiss her.*

MARK. How old are you?

ANGELA (*like she's very old*). Twenty-eight.

MARK. That's not so old.

ANGELA. It's not so young.

MARK. I'm forty-six.

ANGELA. That's not old.

Pause. He kisses her. They kiss for a moment.

I'm sorry. This is kind of weird... I've never been with anybody who was married before.

MARK. We don't have to do anything.

ANGELA. Yeah... I'm sorry. I just feel kind of funny.

MARK. That's all right. I'm not entirely comfortable either, to tell you the truth...

ANGELA. No, but it's fucked up, because I really like you. I really like spending time with you.

MARK. How long were you and Raymond married?

ANGELA. Oh my God, Raymond and I were never married.

MARK. Weren't you? I thought –

ANGELA. Oh my God, he's too unreliable to get married to. Besides, Catholics are not supposed to get divorced. I mean, a lot of people do it. But they're not really supposed to.

MARK. No, I have heard that.

ANGELA. You've heard that, right?

MARK. But isn't it just as bad to live in sin? So to speak? Isn't that as –

ANGELA. Yeah, but you can get forgiven for that. But if you get divorced, they just keep saying like, go back to your husband or you can't get absolution, because they think you didn't really repent. Which, you know, they have a point. Anyway, we should probably get married because of David. But I don't think that's gonna happen right now.

MARK. But might it someday?

ANGELA. Who knows? I don't know what's gonna happen.

Pause. He kisses her again. This goes on for a while.

I don't mean this like it sounds, but would you mind if we go in my room? David has to come through here to use the bathroom...

MARK. Oh – sure. No, of course.

ANGELA. I'm not saying I want to go to bed with you. I just don't want him to...

MARK. No, no, that's fine, of course.

ANGELA. Anyway, I don't have any protection or anything. So –

MARK. That's all right.

ANGELA. Oh no it's not.

MARK. No – I mean, we don't have to do anything.

ANGELA. Okay... Thanks for saying that... I'm gonna get a glass of water. You want something?

MARK. No. Thank you.

ANGELA *exits. We hear running water.* MARK *stands, waiting.* ANGELA *comes back in with the water.*

ANGELA. Okay...!

MARK. Okay.

They go into her bedroom.

Scene Seven

Crossfade to MARK *and* ANNE*'s house.* MARK *crosses into the living room.* ANNE *enters.*

ANNE. Did you see the sketch the guy left for the mantelpiece?

MARK. No. Where is it?

ANNE. It's in the bedroom?

MARK. Oh. No. Should I go look at it right now?

ANNE. No, that's okay. As long as I can call him by tomorrow.

MARK. All right.

ANNE. Plus I think I lost my ATM card. You haven't seen it, have you?

MARK. No.

ANNE. I'm so depressed about it I wanna kill myself. This is the third time in the last six months I've lost my cash card, and I really think sometimes I'm going crazy. I spent the whole afternoon looking for this stupid card, I had seven different errands I was gonna do today and I didn't do any of them and I don't know how I'm gonna do it all tomorrow between the time I get home from work and the time Adam comes home for dinner.

MARK. Can't he order Chinese food?

ANNE. I know he can order Chinese food. I just thought it would be nice if I cooked dinner for him once in a while, instead of always ordering out and feeding him Chinese food and pizza. Other people manage to go to work and make dinner and not lose their cash card and not spend their lives running around like a chicken with its head cut off and still not get anything done, ever.

MARK. I'm sure a lot of people feel that way.

ANNE. That's *their* problem. (*Pause*)

MARK. You look very pretty.

ANNE. Thank you.

MARK. Would you like to have a date with me one of these days?

ANNE. I'd love to.

MARK. When can we do that?

ANNE. Well, you have class on Tuesday and Thursday, and then
    my sister's coming over on Wednesday…

MARK. Uh-huh…

ANNE. And then Friday you said you had something…

MARK (*he's meeting* ANGELA). Oh. Yeah… But –

ANNE. And then Saturday we're all going out to your mother's.
    And then it's Sunday, and you know Adam's gonna want help
    with his English paper at six o'clock on Sunday night, and then
    you're gonna want to watch the baseball game –

MARK. No I'm not.

ANNE. Why don't we forget it.

MARK. First of all, there is no game I care about on Sunday night.

ANNE. All right:

MARK. And I don't see why Adam can't do his homework earlier
    in the day so he doesn't hijack our evening.

ANNE. Because he won't.

MARK. Then let him not do it!

ANNE. Let's just go out next week.

MARK. All right. (*Pause*)

ANNE. What are you doing after class on Friday?

MARK (*a lie*). I'm having drinks with Ben Rothberg. Apparently
    there's a new slot opening up with the project.

ANNE. Really?

MARK. Yeah. This kid they hired had to drop out because they just
    found out his wife has brain cancer –

ANNE. Oh my God.

MARK. Yeah, thirty-one years old –

ANNE. God!

MARK. Anyway, so he dropped out and now there's this availability.

ANNE. What's the position?

MARK. Well – Are you really asking?

ANNE. Yes.

MARK. All right: you remember the project is a large-scale attempt to measure the size of the universe...?

ANNE. Yes, it always sounds like a metaphor for something.

MARK. It's not.

ANNE. No of course not.

MARK. They're trying to measure the size of the universe. The actual size. Not the metaphorical size. Not the size as it relates to our hopes and dreams. The size.

ANNE. All right, take it easy.

MARK. Anyway, the idea is to map the three-dimensional structure of the universe by measuring the red shifts of all the galaxies we can see moving away from the Earth...

ANNE (*lost*). Right.

MARK. The *degree* of red shift in the spectrum of any luminous object tells you how fast the object is moving away from you...

ANNE. That is so true.

MARK. Do you remember any of this?

ANNE. I remember the project has something to do with Outer Space.

MARK. Yes. It has something to do with Outer Space. The main idea is that if we knew how fast the universe was expanding we could make a reasonable calculation as to its size. So Herschel and Ben and the rest of them will be going down to Hawaii and Chile and various observatories around the world to collect new data and new red shifts. And *my* job would involve going through all the catalogues which give the red shifts that have already been measured, and entering them into a computer database. For which I believe it's fair to say that I am overqualified.

ANNE. So you mean physically going through catalogues, looking up numbers and putting them in a computer…?

MARK (*nodding*). Mm-hm. That's right.

ANNE. How many numbers are there to look up?

MARK. Um – About half a million.

ANNE. Gee.

MARK. Well, that's how things get done.

ANNE. Uh-huh. And would you be interested in doing that?

MARK. Um – yes. I would do that. (*Pause*) I realize it sounds slightly boring.

ANNE (*gently*). It does sound a *little* boring…

MARK. Yes. I'm aware of that. However –

ANNE. But does it involve any… Is there any chance of moving into more… other areas?

MARK. I don't really know. Generally speaking, the 'data analyst' is usually a grad student, or a team of grad students. It does have to be done right, but it's not exactly skilled labor.

ANNE. Uh-huh?

MARK. But it's a very respectable, internationally funded long-term project, with a lot of very interesting people working on it… So I don't – I'm hopeful that it's, well, that it's a foot in the door.

ANNE. So this could be really exciting.

MARK. I don't think it's very exciting. I think there's a vague possibility that it might turn into something interesting several years from now, if I'm willing to sit in a room and punch numbers into a computer eight hours a day for the next three or four years.

ANNE. Then why do you want it?

MARK. I don't know that I do. Because it would mean I was part of something.

ANNE. You're a part of something now.

MARK *doesn't answer.*

Scene Eight

Crossfade to MARK's *classroom.* MARK *enters, in his coat, with his briefcase.* ARNOLD *comes in quickly.*

ARNOLD. Hey, did you ever talk to Rothberg yet?

MARK. No. I'm having lunch with him on Friday.

ARNOLD. Well, he's upstairs in Neil's office right now. You want me to send him down?

MARK. Oh – no – I don't think so. I'd rather talk to him on Friday.

ARNOLD. Did you tell him why you wanted to see him?

MARK. Uh, no, I thought I'd –

ARNOLD. See? That's nuts. He could fill the slot by Friday, man. It's not that hard to fill. You want to come up with me now?

MARK. Oh no. No, I don't want to do that…

ARNOLD. Okay, so look: I'll mention very casually you're down here if he wants to say hello.

MARK. All right. Thank you.

ARNOLD. No problem. But – I gotta say – You should be doing this yourself. I mean, you shouldn't require me doing this.

MARK. I'm not requiring you to do anything.

ARNOLD. That's not what I mean. I want to help you if you want the job. What I mean is you really shouldn't have to be encouraged more than a reasonable amount to go after it properly. (*Pause*)

MARK (*very offended*). All right.

ARNOLD. All I mean is I've done this with people before, and if it gets to the point where people have to twist your arm just to get you to take the basic steps necessary to get what you say you want – that doesn't usually work out for anybody. That's all I mean. But then don't sit around and feel bad that it didn't just magically drop in your lap, and then make comments to me about not liking your classes and me having other irons in the fire.

MARK. You know what Arnold? I'll call him tonight myself.

ARNOLD. But why are you offended?

MARK. I don't expect it to drop in my lap. I don't want to go up there twenty minutes before class. I'd like to be as comfortable as possible when I speak to him, and if he comes down here now, I won't be.

ARNOLD. It's just little Benny Rothberg from New Haven. He's not the Great and Powerful Oz. Let me go get him. It's not that big a deal.

MARK. All right… I know you mean well. I think you make a valid point. And I certainly appreciate all your –

ARNOLD. Oh screw that.

ARNOLD goes out. MARK takes out his class materials. IAN enters.

IAN. Professor Williams?

MARK. Yes. Hello. Come in. Am I – what time is it?

IAN. Oh, it's early, it's only six.

MARK. Oh… Are you –

IAN. I was hoping to catch you here before class. I'm in your six-thirty class…? My name is Ian?

MARK. Yes. Hello. What brings you here at this… so early, um, Ian?

IAN is removing a folder from his backpack. From the folder he removes two copies of a short document, one white, one yellow.

IAN. Actually, I meant to come earlier, but I got stuck on the train for like twenty minutes. So I'm gonna probably have to like *rush through* this. Which is like, totally unfair to you, but these things do happen.

MARK. Am I… I'm a little confused…

IAN. Don't worry. I'm totally getting ahead of myself. Okay, Ian: Back up! (*Takes a big breath, exhales.*) I take a fair number of classes like this one, all over the city, pretty much year-round. And I find a lot of the teachers I meet really appreciate a little feedback about their teaching. I know a lot of the institutions provide you with like a one-page comment sheet at the end of the course, but I find that so summary. Somebody takes three hours a week to try to teach me something, it feels really disrespectful to me to just dash off some half-formed opinions on the last day and then *present* that to him as my comments, you know?

MARK. Mm-hm?

IAN. So what I traditionally do is just write up a little critique of the class overall and then go over it with the teacher roughly midway through the course, so they can have a chance to incorporate any of the criticisms they see fit into the rest of the course, and I wanted to go over some of it with you now, if that's okay.

MARK. Oh. Well. That sounds… Actually, to tell you the truth, I am expecting someone in a few minutes –

IAN. Okay. Well look: Let's just get started, and when they get here I'll just go get a tea or something. Okay?

MARK. Um – Yes, all right. Why not?

IAN. Excellent. So –

MARK. You may fire when ready.

IAN. All right. So, I kind of break these down into different categories, so… 'One: Presentation of Information. Excellent.' See, you're doing really well so far.

MARK. Well. Thank you.

IAN (*refers to his notes*). It seems you have an excellent grasp of your subject, and I really admire the way you present the information step by step – and don't jump ahead too much. You have a very good sense of when we're ready for the next step, and when we need to explore an area more thoroughly before arriving at a firm grasp of the material.

MARK. Well, I'm very glad.

IAN. Yeah. Okay. 'Two: Individual Attention.' (*Pause*) Yeah. (*Pause*) This was a tough one for me, because I can really see how courteous you are with the students: you listen carefully, you try to answer on their level… But I gotta say, like, a lot of times I would ask you a question which you thought was like, jumping ahead – maybe because I'm a little better acquainted with some of the basics of astronomy than some of the other people in the class – and you'll say you're gonna deal with my question later. And like, you never do. (*Pause*)

MARK. Oh. Well –

IAN. Like one time early on, I asked you a question about the formation of the different planets in the Solar System? And you were like, 'Wait, wait, I'll tell you later,' and even though you *kind of* answered the question a little later, during a presentation of some other information, you weren't really addressing *my* question. So, for Individual Attention, I gave you a 'Poor.' 'Dissatisfactory' is the worst one. 'Poor' is like the second worst. (*Pause*)

MARK. Well, but, if you say I covered the information…

IAN. Yeah, but by the time you happened to mention it in the regular material, I wasn't really paying attention anymore, so I completely missed it. Poor.

MARK. Yes, well, but don't you think that might suggest some small failure on your part, as the student?

IAN. Um, no. Because a student's natural state of rest is a wandering mind. And it's up to the teacher to reach in and draw focus. Which in this case you really didn't. Something to think about. 'Three: Personal Teaching Style.'

MARK. Listen – Ian –

IAN. Again, this is a really tough one. Style is probably the most personal element a teacher will ever bring to bear on his or her work. So please don't take this personally, but overall, I have to say, I find your style very dry. I think the class suffers badly from a lack of vivacity. There's a kindness and a sincerity to your personality that's really endearing, but I have to say, it's not enough to hold my attention for the duration of a three-hour class. Your jokes are like, so-so. It's more like I'm appreciating the fact that you're trying to make one than I'm really laughing at the actual joke. And I really think you can do better without becoming unnaturally flamboyant. A style must reflect the individual truthfully, otherwise it's either derivative, or reactive. So what you would need to do, I would say, is find some way of infusing your personal style with a little of the inner feeling you seem to have for your subject. Do you see what I mean?

MARK. Um, Ian, I really do have to get ready for the class. Do you want to tell me what my style rating is and then we can continue this some other time?

IAN. Okay. I was going to give you a 'Poor,' but I realized that I might be being overly influenced by my personal taste. Like, a lot of the other students are just not in to you. They think you're too lackluster, or whatever. But there's a father and a son: they sit in the back? They love you. They like want to get to *know* you. So then I thought, when you add it all up, your personal attributes definitely count for something in this cruel world. And I think 'Poor' just doesn't reflect the objective truth. So I gave you a 'Fair.' Four:

MARK. I'm sorry. May I ask, how many more categories are there?

IAN. Um, a few. But if we don't get through the whole thing, that's okay – This is your copy – No – the yellow one. The yellow one.

MARK. I see. All right. I actually am expecting someone in a few minutes... Do you want to leave that with me and I'll just look over the rest of it a little later on?

IAN. Um – yeah, okay.

MARK. The yellow one is my copy?

IAN. Yeah. Here.

IAN *gets up, puzzled.*

Do you want to discuss any of the points we've gone over so far? Because they aren't like, set in stone or anything.

MARK. No. You've... I... You've given me a lot to think about. Particularly in regard to not following up on your questions, I think that's quite valid, and I'll... really do my best to... do better there.

IAN. See – That makes me feel like *I've* helped *you* with something.

MARK. I didn't ask for a full-blown critique of the class at this point... I don't know what I can do about my personal style. I am who I am, and... If the, uh, the father and the –

IAN. Hey, you don't have to defend yourself, Mr Williams, this is just one person's opinion –

MARK. No – I will defend myself… If the father and the son in the back of the class are the only ones who care for my presentational style, perhaps the rest of you will have to be satisfied with having learned something about astronomy, and we can leave style to television situation comedies.

IAN. I'm just trying to draw a connection between a teacher's supposed personal style, and the amount of information his students absorb, that's all. (*Pause*) I hope I haven't –

MARK. No. No. You're a very bright, and you're a thoughtful young man. And what you're, uh, what you've presented to me here shows a serious degree of real, of serious consideration. I'm sure you'll do very well in the world, if somebody doesn't, uh, gun you down in the street first. Now if you don't mind, I'd like to get on with the preparation for my class.

IAN. Okay. And just so you know, I traditionally go through the whole thing all over again at the end of the course. Just so you can feel like you had a chance to make any adjustments that you feel are important…

MARK. So that's a kind of goal I can set for myself.

IAN. Only if you find it useful.

MARK. All right. I think that's enough for one session. Why don't you, um – go. And I'll try to prepare for tonight's ordeal.

IAN. Oh – I hope you don't see it that way.

MARK. No no, not at all.

IAN. I hope *I* haven't made you see it that way.

MARK. No no. I'm only joking.

IAN. See? That was funny.

MARK *does not respond*.

All right. So I'm gonna get a tea… Do you want anything…? Can I –

MARK. No. Thank you.

IAN. No hard feelings.

He offers his hand. MARK *shakes it cursorily.*

MARK. No. Of course not. Okay.

IAN. See you in a bit.

IAN *goes out.* MARK *walks around the room.*

MARK. Fuck you.

He sits at his desk and picks up the yellow copy of the report. He looks through it.

(*Reading aloud.*) 'On balance, despite the occasional rhetorical flourish, I have to say it is truly amazing how anyone could possibly take such an incredibly pedestrian approach to what has to be the single most awe-inspiring subject of them all. But you do. Almost as if you thought the stars themselves were boring.'

End of Act One.

ACT TWO

Scene One

ANGELA*'s apartment. Night.* MARK *and* ANGELA *are in her living room. She's in pajamas. He's partly dressed, and barefoot.*

MARK. No, my father wasn't religious. He was a devout atheist.

ANGELA. Devout atheist!

MARK. That's right. He was a small-town pharmacist. Worked in the local drug store for eighteen years. Old-school Liberal. Hated Richard Nixon above all others. Hated Clinton. I remember sitting there with Dad watching President Clinton at Nixon's funeral on television last year… Did you watch any of that?

ANGELA. No… Not really… A little…

MARK. Well, my dad was very ill at the time, but he insisted on watching the entire funeral because he was so happy that Nixon was dead, except Clinton was ruining it for him. I keep thinking of him at the oddest times. I'll occasionally have insomnia… I've had it pretty badly lately… and I'll be lying there, and I'll suddenly think about my dad. He had these very large, powerful hands, and the few times he lost his temper with me when I was a kid he would grip me by the arm or the elbow, and it was like being gripped by a giant steel pincer. I keep remembering a moment where we were in the hospital, and he was in a wheelchair, waiting for an X-ray, I think it was; and he couldn't get up out of the chair himself. So I took his hand to help him up, and it was the most peculiar sensation. There was the same big meaty hand, there was absolutely no strength in it whatsoever. And when he tried to pull himself up it was as if all the strings inside him had been cut. (*Pause*) I don't know how I got on this topic.

ANGELA. That's all right.

MARK. But I'll – Oh yes. Okay: So I'll be lying there, experiencing a sort of silent movie of all these scenes from his life, and from his illness. And I'll suddenly have a very sharp distinctive feeling that he's there.

ANGELA. Oh yeah, I know what you mean.

MARK. I know it's an illusion, but I'll feel his presence, right there in the room with me. And I've even – once or twice – I've actually spoken to him. Found myself saying, 'Is that you?' Or, 'If you're there, I love you.' Or, 'If that's you, hello. I hope you're there.'

ANGELA. But how do you know he's not there?

MARK. Oh. Well, I don't, of course. But I have no reason to believe he is...

ANGELA. He's there. He's watching you.

MARK. You mean right now?

ANGELA. I don't know right now, but he's watching you. I know my grandmother's watching me. I know she's still there. Your father's there.

MARK. Well... maybe.

ANGELA. You don't think he is?

MARK. It would certainly be nice...

ANGELA. So you're totally an atheist.

MARK. Yes.

ANGELA. So what do you believe in?

MARK. What do I believe in?

ANGELA. Yeah. (*Pause*)

MARK. Well – it's rather a large question.　　ANGELA. You just think it's all random? I'm sorry.

MARK. That's all right. (*Pause*) I don't believe there's any particular *plan* for us, if that's what you mean. (*Pause*) I don't think we are here by any specific design –

ANGELA. But our bodies have a specific design.

MARK. Yes, that's true:

ANGELA. Every blade of grass has a specific design. Every speck of dust. Everything.

MARK. Yes, I – That's what
I've spent my life studying,
one way or another...   ANGELA. I'm sorry.

MARK. No no, there's a *physical* design...

ANGELA. So you believe in one kind of design, but not another?

MARK. Yes, I don't think there's –

ANGELA. It's not like I'm some big Catholic.

MARK. Oh, no –

ANGELA. Obviously. I'm like, sitting here cheating on the father of my illegitimate son with a married man. So. That's like four sins at once, if I believed in it that strictly. To me it's not really about that. It's more like an instinct you have. You know what I mean? It's more like a feeling you have inside. I know you can't prove it.

MARK. Mm-hm?

ANGELA. To me it's more like, it's more like everything that's beautiful. Like... I don't know, like music... or making love, or – I don't know – being with David, or like... I don't know: You know what I mean?

MARK. Mm-hm? I do, yes.

ANGELA. I always think of it like music. Like you can't explain why music makes you feel so good, but it does.

MARK. Well, they do have some idea why people respond to music... There's something in our brains that responds to, um, to different rhythms...

ANGELA. Yeah, but you can't explain why something's a good song or not. Or a good symphony, or whatever.

MARK. Well, it's got nothing in particular to do with one kind of music over another...

ANGELA. No, but I'm just saying more in general: Like, you're saying you only believe in something you can prove. I'm just saying there's a lot more things you *can't* prove, so why don't you believe in *that*?

MARK (*confused*). Why don't I...

ANGELA. If you only believe in what's in front of you, I'm saying there's a million things in front of you that you can't prove. So why don't you believe in them too?

MARK. I do. If I understand you correctly...

ANGELA. But then so how can you say you know your father's not watching?

MARK. I don't know. I don't think he is.

ANGELA. Even though you just told me how you thought he was in the room with you?

MARK. I'm sure there's an explanation for it.

ANGELA. I'm not trying to pick a fight.

MARK. No, I know that.

ANGELA. You just want me to agree with you?

MARK. Not at all.

ANGELA. What do you want?

MARK. How do you mean?

ANGELA. What do you want with me?

MARK. How did we get to that – ?

ANGELA. You just want to talk to your wife and then come over here and go to bed with me?

MARK. No. I don't want to talk to her either. We don't talk about the cosmos: We talk about dry cleaning.

ANGELA. All right.

MARK. I don't like to have these huge sweeping discussions. I don't understand them. I don't think that everyone who's ever died is floating around in their pure form watching over us. I don't. But it's sheer speculation because nobody knows anything about it.

ANGELA. Okay, but look: I know you're gonna laugh at this, but right before my grandmother died, I said, 'When you get to the other side you gotta send me a sign.' And now a lot of times when I'm thinking about her, like my sister and me will get a sign at the same time, when she's in her house and I'm in my house. It happened a lot more right after she died, like the lights would go off and on for no reason in both our houses, or her picture would fall off the wall out of nowhere, right when I would be talking about her... A lot of things happened. You would probably say it was all a coincidence, but I know it was her. Like I know she loved me. And I know that part of her is still here.

MARK. Yes, I think about my father too. And sometimes when I'm thinking about him the phone rings, and it's one of my sisters, and she was thinking about him too. And then other times I'll be thinking about him and the phone doesn't ring. Or it rings and it has nothing to do with him. And sometimes the wind blows, and sometimes the fuse blows out, and sometimes it doesn't. Most of the time it doesn't. I don't think it's true. I don't think my father is watching me, except in my imagination. I could certainly be wrong.

ANGELA. So you think we're just alone?

MARK. Yes. I do.

ANGELA. Do you feel alone when you're with me?

MARK. No, I don't.

ANGELA. Well that's good anyway... I guess. (*Pause*) Anyway... I gotta get up really early...

MARK. All right.

ANGELA. I'm not trying to kick you out: I got two ten-hour shifts this weekend... But it's almost over!

MARK. No, I should get going myself.

He is looking for his shoes and socks.

ANGELA. What are you looking for?

MARK. My shoe.

ANGELA. It's right here.

MARK. Thank you.

He sits down and puts on his shoes. She watches him.

ANGELA. I didn't mean to make you uncomfortable…

MARK. You haven't. (*Stands.*) All right. I'll call you tomorrow.

ANGELA. Yeah but do you love me?

MARK *hesitates.*

Mark. Relax. I'm just kidding.

MARK. I know you're kidding…

ANGELA. Why? What were you going to say?

MARK *does not respond.*

What were you going to say…?

MARK *does not respond.*

Scene Two

Crossfade to MARK'*s living room.* MARK *comes in and takes his coat off. Very loud electric guitar can be heard through the walls.* MARK *opens the basement door.*

MARK. Adam? (*Pause*) ADAM!

The music stops.

ADAM (*off*). *WHAT?*

MARK *slams the door shut.*

(*Off, muffled.*) What is your *problem*?

MARK *yanks open the door again.*

MARK. I don't have a problem. It's ten o'clock at night!

ADAM (*off*). I'm trying to get a level! I didn't even know you were home!

MARK. We have neighbors, Adam!

ADAM (*off*). So? Why are you so obsessed with what the neighbors think?

MARK. I'm not obsessed with what the neighbors think. I could hear you halfway down the block. Through the windows of my car!

ADAM (*off*). But how do you know they weren't enjoying it?

MARK. Because it's nearly impossible!

ADAM (*off*). Look, I'm sorry your life hasn't worked out the way you wanted it to, but you don't have to take it out on me.

MARK (*livid*). Don't say anything else to me. Practice your guitar if that's what you're going to do. Only don't say anything else to me.

ADAM (*off*). You're sick.

MARK. No you're sick!

MARK *slams the basement door. His hands are shaking. He goes to the stereo system. He picks a CD and puts on the aria 'Di provenza il mar' from* La Traviata. *He mixes himself a drink and sits down. At the end of the first stanza he has had enough and he gets up quickly and takes it off, just as* ANNE *comes in the front door.*

ANNE. Hi.

MARK. Hello.

ANNE. What's the matter?

MARK. Nothing. How are you?

ANNE. I'm okay. When did you get back?

MARK. A little while ago.

ANNE. How'd it go?

MARK. I think it went well.

ANNE. Good. I want to hear about it. Hold on.

She exits and then comes back, minus her coat.

So what did he say? Tell me all about it.

MARK. It went well. He's going to let me know.

ANNE. But you thought it went well?

MARK. Yes. It sounded very positive. I still have to have a serious discussion with the school and the Planetarium about my class load... But I think it looks pretty good.

ANNE. God. I think that's really great! So encouraging.

MARK. Very encouraging.

ANNE. Now. I have to tell you something. And I don't want you to get mad.

MARK. All right.

ANNE. I talked to my mother...

MARK. Oh, about the trip?

ANNE. Oh yes. Are you ready for this?

MARK. I don't know.

ANNE. She wants to bring Eleanor and Eleanor's son. Rob.

MARK. Rob? The one we met?

ANNE. Yes.

MARK. She wants to bring him?

ANNE. Yes.

MARK. He's in his fifties.

ANNE. Don't panic...

MARK. You don't *bring* your fifty-year-old son.

ANNE. She wants to bring him *along*.

MARK. I don't understand. Does she have a car seat for him? How's she going to bring him?

ANNE. I know, I know, but listen. This is pretty good. She wants to bring Eleanor and Rob, and they all want to stay here.

MARK. Where are we going to put them?

ANNE. That's what I said. But she said she and Eleanor can share the guest room and Rob can sleep out here.

MARK. Rob can sleep out here?

ANNE. It's only for a few nights.

MARK. But I don't understand. Why can't they stay in a hotel? I don't mean to be disagreeable…

ANNE. I don't know –

MARK. I think that's asking a lot.

ANNE. I know. It's just that she and I had already discussed her and Eleanor staying here, and I told her that one of them could sleep on the pullout sofa –

MARK. No, Anne. I don't – No.

ANNE. Just calm down. I already told her we could put up the two of them and that one of them could sleep out here, but then she mentioned this about bringing Rob and said she and Eleanor could sleep in the same bed in the spare room. So I didn't know how to tell her that we were willing to put either her or Eleanor on the pullout sofa, but not Rob.

MARK. Because your mother and Eleanor are teeny tiny cute little old ladies and Rob is a big fat disgusting middle-aged man, that's why. I don't know a nice way to say it.

ANNE. He's not that fat!

MARK. He's not thin. We don't even know him!

ANNE. Yes we do, Mark. We met him the last time we went to Pennsylvania?

MARK. Yes. I remember –

ANNE. He's an art dealer. Remember we saw his gallery? It had all those clown pictures in it?

MARK. Yes, I remember him perfectly. I have no objection to his intrinsic value as a human being. I still don't want someone I barely know sleeping in my living room because he and his mother are too cheap to stay in a hotel.

ANNE. Why don't I tell her not to come.

MARK. Why don't you *not* tell her not to come? Why don't you tell her we'd like to have her, but it's too many people for us to put up, and we'd be very happy to help them to find a nice, cheap, clean hotel.

ANNE. Why don't *you* tell her?

MARK. I'd be very happy to. I think it's an imposition!

ANNE. But we're gonna be with them anyway! And what's the difference at the end of the night when we go to bed, if he pulls out the sofa? And when we get up in the morning he folds up the sofa and we all have breakfast and it's exactly the same? Why do you have to be so incredibly inhospitable?

MARK. I don't think I am!

ANNE. My mother is seventy-nine years old! I see her *twice a year*! And if she wants to bring her friends it's just not that big a deal! Tell you what. Why don't you go up to Connecticut that weekend and see *your* mother, and then you don't have to see any of them!

MARK. Because that would be rude.

ANNE. It's rude to make somebody stay in a hotel when you have plenty of room to put them up yourself. And if you were willing to let Eleanor sleep on the sofa I don't see that you have a leg to stand on!

MARK. We *don't* have plenty of room.

ANNE. But if you want to call   MARK. Yes. Yes. Okay. Yes.
my mother – If you want to
call up my mother and tell
her they can't stay here,
be my guest.

MARK. All right. I will.

ANNE. Just remember that if you do we will be hearing about it for the rest of our lives.

MARK (*muttering*). You should have said no to her in the first place.

ANNE. What did you say?

MARK. Nothing.

ANNE. No: what did you say?

MARK. I said you should have said no to her in the first place.

ANNE. And not have let her visit? Not have let my mother visit?

MARK. No, and not have brought Eleanor! I don't want to talk about this anymore!

ANNE. But I *asked* you about that! I *asked* you about it!

MARK. I really cannot discuss this anymore.

ANNE. And I couldn't get two words out of my mouth before you started moaning and groaning and telling me that you didn't care and that whatever I did was fine and how you didn't want to talk about it! So I told her to bring Eleanor because she was obviously very excited about the idea of bringing her – and you said that *whatever I wanted to do was fine with you*!

MARK. Look – Listen –

ANNE. And then today she	MARK. Please. Please. –
mentioned the idea of	Just tell them it's fine.
bringing Rob! I didn't	They can all stay here.
know what to say! I didn't	It's fine.
tell her it was okay yet!	I take it back. I take it back.

MARK *sits down. Silence.*

ANNE. What were you listening to when I came in?

MARK. It's… That song I like, from *La Traviata*. (*A joke:*) The opera.

ANNE. Yes, I'm familiar with it.

MARK. It's… Alfredo's father comes to persuade Violetta to give him up, to give up Alfredo, because his daughter is getting married and if Alfredo keeps living with Violetta the family will be ruined. And the daughter will never be able to marry. So Violetta agrees to leave Alfredo, and she writes him a note and leaves before he comes home. And then Alfredo comes home and finds the note and he's in despair. And he sees his father there, at the house. And his father sings to him, while Alfredo is heartbroken. He sings to him thanking God for giving him back his son. He says, 'Don't you remember how happy you were at

home?' And then he sings how he would thank God if Alfredo
came back home with him, but meanwhile Alfredo's heart is
breaking because he doesn't have Violetta anymore.

ANNE. Why did you put that on? Because you were thinking of
your dad?

MARK. I suppose so. I always think of that song.

ADAM's guitar starts up again offstage, much lowered.

And that's a very beautiful song as well. My *God* he's gifted.

ANNE. What am I going to do?

MARK. Tell them they can come. It's all right. I'm sorry.

ANNE. Do you still care about me at all?

MARK. Of course I do. Of course I do.

He hugs her, but it's a little strained.

What did you do today?

ANNE. Oh. Worked. Shopped. Talked to the guy about the
mantelpiece.

MARK. Oh yes. What did you decide?

ANNE. I think we should let him build it.

MARK. All right, good. (*A joke:*) I support you in this as in every
other decision.

ANNE. Yeah, right.

MARK *turns on the TV.*

MARK. Look, honey. It's Humphrey Bogart. My alter ego.

We hear some dialogue from The Big Sleep.

EDDY MARS (*on TV*). Is that any of your business?

MARLOWE (*on TV*). I could make it my business.

EDDY MARS (*on TV*). I could make your business my business.

MARLOWE (*on TV*). You wouldn't like it, the pay's too small.

ANNE. Hey, you want to fool around?

MARK. All right.

ANNE. I'll meet you upstairs.

MARK. All right.

ANNE opens the basement door. MARK continues to watch TV.

ANNE (*to* ADAM). Adam? I don't want to cramp your style, but I think it's getting a little late for that. Do you think you could wrap it up in a few minutes or use the headphones?

ADAM (*off*). No problem, Mom. Thank you for asking so politely.

ANNE. You're welcome.

She closes the basement door.

(*To* MARK.) Don't be too long. I have to get up really early tomorrow. And I don't want to have to rush.

MARK. All right.

She exits. He flips the channels. Stops at the news.

BRITISH TV NARRATOR....testimony describing hundreds of refugees without access to water or medical supplies. Other refugees tell stories of Serb soldiers executing large numbers of male villagers in the woods outside their village. This thirteen-year-old boy showed us the last place he says he saw his father and four younger brothers alive –

MARK changes the channel.

MOVIE COMMERCIAL ANNOUNCER. Experience the movie critics across the country are calling one of the most extraordinary films in a decade –

MARK turns off the TV. He goes to the basement door and opens it.

MARK. Adam?

ADAM (*off*). Yes?

MARK. I apologize for losing my temper. I still think the music was too loud, but I know you didn't realize anyone was home, and I'm sorry.

ADAM (*off*). I'm sorry too.

MARK. Thank you.

ADAM (*off*). Goodnight, Dad.

MARK. Goodnight, son.

MARK *closes the door. The guitar starts up again.*

Scene Three

Crossfade to NORMAN*'s hospital room.* ANGELA *is sitting with* NORMAN. NORMAN *is a little delirious. His eyes are sometimes closed and sometimes open.*

NORMAN. The Liberals love Clinton... They're so desperate. They don't get it. They're such suckers. They're so complacent and stupid. Clinton's such a chickenshit. Look at the girls he dates. If just once he would just step up and try to fuck somebody who makes over twenty thousand dollars a year I think he could be a really great man.

ANGELA. Try and relax a little, Norman.

NORMAN. I remember in the eighties everybody was writing articles about how the balance of global power was going to have shifted to Asia by now, absolutely. Have you noticed that, Angela? How the balance of global power has shifted over to the Asian rim? I haven't either. You know why? Because nobody knows what the fuck they're talking about, that's why. I met a guy from England last year who told me that by the year 2000 there'll be so many Latinos in the Southwestern United States there'll be a massive movement to secede from the union. I listened to this guy for twenty minutes and I thought, Gee, I didn't know that. And he said, Yeah, look at the statistics. It's going to tip the whole population down there, Texas, Arizona, New Mexico – they're all gonna secede from the United States. And then I thought, No they're *not*. They're not gonna leave their families and risk their lives to come here and risk getting deported all day long so they can secede from the United States and start another Central American country. And

I said that to this guy, and he said, Oh yeah, I guess not, probably not. I mean what the fuck is this guy talking about?

ANGELA. Are you in pain, Norman?

NORMAN. Not at all. No.

ANGELA. Okay.

NORMAN. I love morphine. I would like to marry it.

She goes to the refrigerator to get him some ginger ale.

I mean it's easy for me to say send the Marines to Kosovo. I don't have to go. I didn't join the Marines. My brother was in the Marines.

ANGELA. The one who lives in Cincinnati? I didn't know that.

NORMAN. No, no, my other brother. Owen. The one who died.

ANGELA. Oh he died? What happened to him?

NORMAN. He was shot in World War Two.

ANGELA. Oh no really? That's terrible.

NORMAN. We think he was shot. That's what my dad told us, but it's a little vague. I have a feeling he was really blown apart, because we were never allowed to see his body. I guess it doesn't matter anymore.

ANGELA. Was that your older brother?

NORMAN. Yeah. God he was a good athlete. Holy cow. He could really throw a baseball. Wonderful talent. He was good at any sport. Great eyesight. Great reflexes.

ANGELA. God, that's so sad. How old was he?

NORMAN. Oh, you know, he was nineteen. Nineteen fucking years old I worshipped him. I miss him like it was fucking yesterday. (*Starts to cry.*) I'm seventy-two and I still think of him as older than me. You know, when I picture him in my mind. I guess you always do.

ANGELA. Here. Have some of this.

She brings him a can of ginger ale with a straw sticking out of it.

NORMAN. I don't want it.

ANGELA. Come on, just try a little.

NORMAN. Take it away, I can't do it. I don't want to do it anymore. I'm trying to put on a good show, but I wish they'd just let me go. There's no point anymore, sweetheart. Even if I got better my body is a wreck. I'll never get up and down the stairs. I can't say any of this to them, okay? I'm sorry.

ANGELA. It's okay.

NORMAN. I'd like to go for a walk or sit on the porch or something. Smell some fresh air. You know what I mean?

ANGELA. Sure I do. You will. You still have a good chance, Norman.

NORMAN. Give me a break. I'm practically dead already.

ANGELA. That's not true. You just gotta wait.

NORMAN. I just gotta wait…

NORMAN *is drifting off*. DORIS *comes in*.

ANGELA. Hi Doris.

DORIS. Hello Angela.

ANGELA. Norman, Doris just came in. (*Pause*) Norman, Doris is here.

DORIS. Is he asleep?

ANGELA. Yeah… He's been kind of in and out today…

DORIS. Can I talk to you for a minute please?

ANGELA. Sure.

They step away from the bed.

DORIS. Listen. This is a little uncomfortable for me, but the last time you were here, Angela, I came into the room and I saw you kissing my father.

ANGELA. Oh… No –

DORIS. Yes. I did. Yes. I did. I came into the room and you were leaned over the bed and you were kissing him. Now –

ANGELA. Oh that was –

DORIS. No, just let me finish. My father is very sick. He may not make it through the *week*. I know you and he have this little flirtation going, and that's okay within limits. But he's a very sick man and I – I just don't understand it. I don't understand it.

ANGELA. It wasn't anything, Doris. He was feeling really bad that day –

DORIS. I don't care how bad he was feeling! Do you have any idea how inappropriate this is?

ANGELA *does not respond.*

First I walk in the door and he's talking about your ass. And then I hear you talking about his ass, and then I went out again because I wanted to hear where this was going. And then I come into the room and you're leaned over the bed and you're like, making *out* with him! Do you know how much trouble you could be in?

ANGELA. But I wasn't do–

DORIS. I mean is this some kind of turn-on for you to tease a sick old man in a cancer hospital? And how do you know it's not dangerous to his health?

ANGELA. Because I didn't do anything, Doris. I'm really sorry you're upset –

DORIS. What? What are you going to say?

ANGELA. The stuff about him talking about my rear end is just him kidding around. So I probably said something like I was kidding around back, because –

DORIS. But it's so incredibly inappropriate!

ANGELA. ...and then he asked... I said I was leaving and he said, Give me a kiss. Not like 'Give me a big kiss,' but like... I can't explain it. It was like, to comfort him, like a kiss on the cheek.

DORIS. Don't con me, Angela. I *saw* it!

ANGELA. It wasn't on the cheek, but that was the kind of kiss it was.

DORIS. I saw it, Angela. It wasn't on the cheek. And you don't tell a seventy-two-year-old man who's recovering from surgery that you want to be his girlfriend!

ANGELA. But we were just kidding with each other. And that kiss was like – I don't know – like he was challenging me.

DORIS. To do what?

ANGELA. No, not like that sounds…

DORIS. Challenging you to do what? I would really like to hear this!

ANGELA. Not like it sounds, but like – It was nothing. I swear to God it was nothing.

DORIS. Well, you're putting me in a very bad position.

ANGELA. Then maybe you should tell Maureen about it. I'll tell her what happened. Maybe I did something wrong. He was so sad that day. And he was saying how he was so tired of being sick, and when I left the room, he said Give me a kiss. But he's a man. And sometimes they just flirt with you because they don't feel like men anymore. And it's not like I'm gonna do anything, of course not –

DORIS. I just think you're –

ANGELA. But he asked me, and I did it because I love him, and he asked me to. And if you want to tell Maureen, I guess just go ahead and do it. It was such a little thing. It didn't seem like such a big deal. Like: 'Oh, no, no, you're a patient, sorry, no.'

DORIS. Well you're putting me in a bad position. You're putting me in a very bad position and I really resent it. I am dealing with this whole thing nearly single-handed. People come and go all day long, but I'm the one who's here every night, and every morning before I go to work. I have three kids at home with a lot of problems. I have my sister giving me advice – advice! From two thousand miles away! She's been here *once*! He's got twenty different fucking doctors and they're all telling me something different and I cannot deal with this! Are you fucking kidding me?! It's like a sick joke! So, uh, I just gotta think about what I'm gonna do.

ANGELA. Doris, I really want to be a nurse.

DORIS. Oh you do?

ANGELA. I been in school for two years. I've barely seen my little
boy all year because I want to try to get through the program and
get started. I made friends with your father. I thought I made
friends with you and that's all it is. I only did it 'cause I care
about him.

DORIS. Yeah, you know what? That's not your best argument.
(*Bursts into tears.*) I don't know what to do! If his numbers
don't go up he's not gonna be here next week! It's not like we're
all that close!

ANGELA. He's gonna be all right!

DORIS. You don't know that! I fucking hate that! I feel like I'm
going crazy! I'm just trying to take care of him…!

ANGELA. I know you are. You're a good daughter.

DORIS. Oh give me a break! He doesn't even like me!

ANGELA. Yes he does!

DORIS. You hear the way he talks about us! Sanctimonious shit! Oh,
I'm sure he's incredibly charming with everybody else! I know all
about *that*! Boy, do I ever! I don't even know why I come here!
My mother wouldn't have taken any of this shit for five minutes!

DORIS *cries.* ANGELA *reaches out and rubs her shoulder
awkwardly.*

You don't have to do that. It's okay.

ANGELA. Okay, I'm sorry.

ANGELA *draws her hand away instantly.*

DORIS. All right: Now that I've made a complete spectacle of
myself…

ANGELA. No you didn't…

DORIS. I'd like to visit with him for a while now. I honestly don't
know what I'm going to do about this. I can't think about it right
now.

ANGELA. Well… if you want to talk to Maureen about it, I just
wish you would tell me, so I could tell her my side.

DORIS. You know what? I don't want to talk about this anymore. I have more important things on my mind. And right now I'd like to visit with my father if that's okay with you.

ANGELA. All right, of course. I'll see you later.

DORIS. Yeah. So long.

ANGELA lingers, then exits. NORMAN opens his eyes.

NORMAN. Hi.

DORIS. Hi Dad.

NORMAN. How long have you been here?

DORIS. Just a few minutes. Go back to sleep if you want. (*Pause*)

NORMAN (*meaning his condition*). It's not so good.

DORIS. I know.

NORMAN. I'm sorry.

DORIS. Please don't say that!

NORMAN. I love you honey.

DORIS. I love you too...!

She starts crying again and bows her head over his hand.

Scene Four

Crossfade to MARK's classroom. MARK is unpacking his slides. He puts a basketball on the desk. ANGELA comes in, wearing her coat.

MARK (*surprised*). Hello.

ANGELA. Hi.

MARK. What a nice surprise –

She closes the door and kisses him. She opens her coat and puts his hands under her shirt. She sheds her winter coat.

I have class –

She takes MARK*'s jacket off his shoulders and it falls to the floor. He keeps thinking it will stop somewhere but it doesn't. Still kissing him or trying to, she reaches down and tries to take down her pantyhose.*

I have class.

She pushes him down onto the floor behind the desk and climbs on top of him.

ARNOLD *opens the door, knocking. Sees them.*

ARNOLD. Holy shit.

MARK. Oh – that's okay, Arnold.

ARNOLD *exits, closing the door.*

That's bad.

ANGELA. Come on, don't stop, he already saw us. Come on. I love you. Come on.

MARK. No, that's very bad –

ANGELA. I want them to know about it. I want everyone to know about it –

MARK. I think we ought to stop.

ANGELA. Mark, I love you.

MARK. I love you too.

They start kissing again, but he feels awkward.

IAN *knocks on the door and half-opens it.*

IAN. Hello?

MARK. Yeah just a minute…!

IAN (*sees them*). Oh. I am so sorry!

He pulls the door shut.

MARK. I really think we'd better stop.

ANGELA. All right. I'm sorry.

MARK. No no, don't be sorry.

She disengages herself and starts fixing her clothes.

ANGELA. I gotta go anyway. David's with my mother.

MARK. All right... Well... Thanks for stopping by.

ANGELA. If you want, I was gonna send David to Philadelphia this weekend so we could have a date. Aren't I a good mother?

MARK. Don't you have the hospital over the weekend?

ANGELA. Yeah, but he would leave right after school on Friday. So I could see you Friday night if it's not too late. You want me to make you dinner?

MARK. All right. Wonderful.

ANGELA. I could make some lamb chops. Do you like lamp chops?

MARK. Oh yes, very much.

ANGELA. Or I could make a lasagna. That way I could make it the day before, and I won't have to be rushing around.

MARK. Honestly, whatever's easiest.

ANGELA. Maybe the whole thing's really dumb. I mean, how long are we gonna go on like this...?

MARK *does not respond.*

It's not even like I'm looking for anything more right now. I hardly have any time for David, never mind you. You're not gonna leave your family. Even if you wanted to, I don't think you would. Would you? (*Pause*)

MARK. I don't think so, no. Not with a fifteen-year-old kid at home... No.

ANGELA. Okay. That's fine. I don't want you to. I see what David's going through. I got enough on my conscience. I don't wanna be that person. But then what are we doing?

MARK. I don't know... I look forward to seeing you... You're –

ANGELA. So what?

MARK. Let's stop then.

ANGELA. I know you care about me, but it's ugly. It's ugly, Mark, and there's no future. To me that's what makes it ugly even more than that you're married – and I *should* be married, but that's another subject. Plus you see how like David's in love with you.

MARK. With me?

ANGELA. Yeah, because you pay attention to him!

MARK. Well, that's no big effort –

ANGELA. He's always like, 'Where's Mark? Let's hang out with Mark.' And I'm like, 'Oh, we can't this week, baby.' I don't know if he knew what we were *doing*... I'm not saying it to make you feel bad.

MARK. No, you're right. I think you're right.

ANGELA. Then why don't you stop?

MARK. I'm not good at having these conversations. If you don't like it, let's stop. But I do like it and I don't want to stop. I know it's ugly. I feel the same way about it as you do. But my life doesn't just belong to Anne and Adam. I'm forty-six years old, and it is my life partly, at least. I can't defend it. If you want to stop, let's stop. Only don't expect me to be the one to say it.

ANGELA. Well... I just think I wanna cool it for now. All right?

MARK. Yes, of course.

ANGELA. Do you still wanna come for dinner Friday? Even if it's just as friends?

MARK. No, I'd like to.

ANGELA. Just not as much, right?

MARK. Angela, what do you want me to say?

ANGELA. I'm sorry. I'll see you next Friday. Call me first.

MARK. All right. I will.

She kisses him on the cheek and goes out. MARK *fixes himself up.* ARNOLD *comes in again.*

ARNOLD. Hi...

MARK. Hello Arnold. Sorry about that. I realize this is very high school.

ARNOLD. I don't know what high school you went to. The girls at my high school didn't screw the science geeks on the floor of the science lab.

MARK. Well, I'd appreciate it if –

ARNOLD. You've struck a blow for astrophysics that'll reverberate from here to the National Academy of Sciences.

MARK. Obviously I would appreciate it if you would keep this to yourself.

ARNOLD. Oh I don't think so. I don't think you realize what a good story this is. I mean – people don't really think of you this way.

MARK. That's very funny, Arnold. All the same, I'd appreciate it if you wouldn't –

ARNOLD. Oh relax, I'm not gonna say anything. Why would I?

MARK. I don't know. I'm not especially proud of this.

ARNOLD. Why not? *I'm* proud of you.

MARK. What did you want to see me about?

ARNOLD. You know, I really can't remember... Any word from Ben?

MARK. Oh – Yes – I got it.

ARNOLD. What?

MARK. I got the position. He called this morning.

ARNOLD. What? Hey! That's fantastic!

MARK. Thank you.

ARNOLD. What are you talking about, 'thank you?' That's terrific! Let's shake hands! You are having a really good day.

They shake hands.

MARK. Thanks, Arnold. And – thank you for all your support. I do appreciate it...

Pause. ARNOLD *looks at* MARK *for a moment.*

ARNOLD. That's okay. You're kind of a god to me now.

MARK. Arnold, enough.

ARNOLD. Oh come on. You have to admit it's kind of funny.

MARK. I don't think so. (*Pause*)

ARNOLD. Well, it's great news...

MARK. I just hope I can work out my schedule with the college...

ARNOLD. What?

MARK. Well, the salary with Herschel is absolute peanuts.

ARNOLD. Oh you are such a tremendous drag.

MARK. No, I'm not. I have a son who's two years away from college... Not a terrible student, but not great...

ARNOLD. What about a music scholarship?

MARK. I really don't think so.

ARNOLD. No, you had just mentioned he played the guitar.

MARK. No.

MRS PYSNER *comes in.*

Hello.

She doesn't respond. Takes her seat.

ARNOLD. All right... See you later.

He goes out. MARK *is alone with* MRS PYSNER.

MARK. It's really getting to be winter.

She does not respond. IAN *walks in, looking at* MARK *in a new way.*

Hello.

IAN. How's it going?

MARK. Very well, thanks.

IAN. I'm really sorry about before – I thought it was time for class.

MARK. Please – that's quite all right.

IAN. Yeah.

Still looking at MARK, IAN *takes his seat. The other students file in, or there is a light change.* MARK *faces the class and sighs a little.*

MARK. Well: It's nice to see you all again. Before we start tonight, I'd like to address a few helpful criticisms that have come to my attention over the last few weeks. It often happens that we teachers find ourselves becoming a bit isolated over the years, from our students, even from our subject... So what I'd like to do, is to actually – to thank those students in the class who took their lives in their hands and came forward with their concerns about the class, and to promise them that I will do everything in my power to address each and every one of them. And to say for the record, that if I fall short, it will hopefully not be for lack of trying. Now: Tonight we're going to talk about the universe. The universe. So. Before we begin, is there anyone here who doesn't know what the universe is? Who doesn't understand what I mean when I say the word 'universe?'

MRS PYSNER *raises her hand.*

MRS PYSNER. I have a question.

MARK. Yes.

MRS PYSNER. Is the universe inside the galaxy, or is the galaxy inside the universe? (*Pause*) Or is that where the whole Einstein thing comes in? (*Pause*)

MARK. Well... I'm not sure what you mean by the whole Einstein thing...

MRS PYSNER. Albert Einstein? The father of relativity?

MARK. No – I know who he is. Um – But to answer your question: The galaxy is inside the universe. There are billions of galaxies in the universe. Just as there are billions of stars to a galaxy...

MRS PYSNER. Going toward it.

MARK. No... Billions of stars to a galaxy, as there are millions of grains of sands to a beach.

MRS PYSNER. So...

MARK. So, our galaxy is inside the universe. All galaxies are inside the universe. Everything that exists is inside the universe. The universe is as big as it gets. Nothing is bigger than the universe. The universe is all there is. I hope that's clear.

MRS PYSNER. And it's bigger than a galaxy.

MARK. Yes. (*Pause*)

MRS PYSNER (*understands*). Okay.

MARK (*startled*). Good…! Um – Hm…!

He is momentarily thrown. Recovers himself. He picks up the basketball.

Well… Um… Now: suppose this is our Sun:

Scene Five

Crossfade to ANGELA*'s living room. The lights are out or very low.* ANGELA *is lying on her back on the sofa, looking at nothing. She looks awful. The house phone buzzes. It buzzes again.* ANGELA *gets up and hits the intercom.*

ANGELA. Quién es?

MARK (*on the intercom*). Angela, it's Mark. I'd like to talk to you for just five minutes. If it's not a good time just tell me when I can talk to you on the phone. I've been trying to call you for three weeks. I don't want to harass you. But I just want to know that you're all right. And I'd like to talk to you, just briefly – just for my own sake. Um…

She buzzes him in, sits on the sofa and waits. MARK *knocks on the door. She starts to go to the door, turns back to turn on a light, wipes her eyes, goes to the door lets him in.*

I won't stay long. I have a few things I'd like to say.

ANGELA. That's all right.

MARK. Is David home?

ANGELA. No.

MARK. Is he in Philadelphia?

ANGELA. No.

MARK. What's the matter?

ANGELA. Nothing.

MARK. I don't mean to harass you. If you'd rather I didn't call I won't –

ANGELA. Yes. I would rather.

MARK. All right. (*Pause*) I don't suppose I'm entitled to an explanation… But –

ANGELA. I can't talk to you right now.

MARK. All right. (*Pause*) Well. I do wish you would tell me why… Um, but –

ANGELA. Please go away.

MARK. Angela what's the matter?

ANGELA. Please go away. Please go away, Mark.

MARK. I'm not going to go away. I want you to tell me what's wrong. Even if you think I should know without your telling me. Things have fallen apart a bit on my end… It doesn't look like I'm going to be able to take that job after all. The college won't let me reduce my course load –

ANGELA. Please stop. I can't talk to you right now. It's not your fault: just go away. I'm sick. I'm very, very sick. I can't talk to you. Just take my word and go away. Don't call me anymore. I'm not gonna be here anyway. I'm going away. I don't want to see you anymore. I don't want to see you again. I don't want to see anyone ever again. Please don't make me say anything else! If you ever cared about me, I'm begging you! Don't make me say anything else today. I'm going to kill myself.

MARK. What are you talking about? I'm not going to go away just like that. I want you to tell me what you're talking about.

ANGELA. I can't.

MARK. Is it David? Did something happen at the hospital? Is it just – Have you just had enough?

ANGELA. *Please!!!*

MARK. All right. I don't understand… But all right…

ANGELA. They shot him.

MARK. Who? Who shot who?

ANGELA. David.

MARK. What?

ANGELA. They shot him. In Philadelphia. Three weeks ago. It was a gang thing. David and Raymond were going to the movies and a car drove by and tried to shoot this guy who was standing there. But they hit David. He's dead. Raymond was standing right there. They killed some other little girl and David and then they drove away. Please go away now, Mark! Please go away!

MARK. I can't believe it.

ANGELA. I know you can't believe it! But I don't want to talk to you! I would have killed myself three weeks ago, but I'm afraid if I do then I'm gonna go to hell – Okay? And then I'm never gonna see him again! I know you think it's funny! But we shouldn't have ever done what we were doing! He was only nine years old. I don't want to talk to you! I want to be with my family. I want to be with Raymond. I don't ever want to talk to you again. Don't ever come and see me again! I don't want to hear anything you have to say! I don't know what do to. I wish somebody would kill me!

MARK. Oh my God. Oh Angela…

ANGELA. And don't you fucking tell me that I'm never gonna see him again!

MARK. Of course I'm not going to say that!

ANGELA. Because if you say that to me I'm gonna kill myself right in front of you right this minute, I swear to God!

MARK. No, no – ! Of course I'm not going to say that!

She collapses into his arms sobbing.

I'm not going to say that! I don't know anything. You'll see him again. Don't make me go now. You'll see him again. Of course you'll see him again.

ANGELA. My sister's coming over.

MARK. I don't care.

ANGELA. I wish I was dead.

MARK. I know.

ANGELA. What am I gonna do?

MARK. I don't know. I don't know, sweetheart. I don't know what to tell you. I don't know.

Scene Six

Crossfade to MARK*'s house.* MARK *comes in, shell-shocked. He puts down his briefcase, hangs up his winter coat. Stomps slush from his shoes.* ANNE *comes in from the kitchen.*

ANNE. Hi. Where have you been? I was getting kind of worried.

MARK. I'm sorry. I was literally stuck in traffic for an hour and a half.

ANNE. Can you believe this snow?

MARK. No... I can't.

ANNE. You should see the back yard. It's really beautiful.

MARK. I take it they're not here yet?

ANNE. No. I assume they're stuck in traffic too. I kind of wish they weren't driving in this weather. I hope my mother's not driving.

MARK. Whose car are they taking?

ANNE. My mother's.

MARK. Oh good. I wouldn't want Rob and Eleanor to have to absorb the depreciation on the car.

ANNE. God, that is a really funny joke.

MARK. What time were they supposed to get here?

ANNE. Seven-thirty.

MARK. I'm sure they'll be here soon.

ANNE. Well, I think we should probably order. I told them we'd get Chinese food, but I don't even know if they'll deliver in this weather. We might have to go get it.

MARK. I'm sure they'll deliver if they're open.

ANNE. Do you want to call them?

MARK. Yes.

ANNE. Why were you so late?

MARK. I... This has nothing to do with us, but... This woman I know... one of my students... She was going to enroll her son in the kiddie class, and I showed them around the building one time, in September. Anyway, she's a very nice young woman. She's getting her training to be a nurse –

ANNE. I'm sorry: We should order. Because if they're *not* delivering then one of us is gonna have to drive in and pick it up, and if they close at nine-thirty –

The phone rings.

Maybe that's them.

She exits.

(*Off.*) Hello? – Oh, hi, Helen – We're fine, how are you?... No – Helen? Helen? We were gonna drive up and get you on Christmas Eve day, and then we're gonna... Yeah, he just came in. Hold on.

She comes in.

It's your mother.

MARK. I can't talk to her right now.

ANNE. She's asking me about Christmas for the hundredth time.

MARK. Yes, I heard.

ANNE. I think she's really having problems with her memory.

MARK. What do you want me do about it? (*Pause*)

ANNE. Nothing.

She exits.

(*Off.*) Helen, can he call you back?... No, we were always gonna do it this way... Well I can't remember what day it is most of the time, so don't... Okay. He'll call you back.

She enters.

I didn't mean there was anything you should do about it. I just meant I've discussed this with her at least three times and she can't seem to get it straight. You don't have to rip my fuckin' head off!

MARK. I'm sorry.

ANNE. I cannot function if you're gonna snap at me every five minutes! You do it way too much!

MARK. I know. I apologize.

ANNE. Yeah, after a certain point it doesn't help. You just become a serial apologizer.

MARK. Anne, what do you want me to do? I'm trying my level best. I am trying my level best. I...

ANNE. What's the matter?

MARK. I'm trying to tell you about this thing that happened. This woman in my class and her son that I was trying to tell you about.

ANNE. Okay.

MARK. I got to know them a little this semester, I got know her son a little, because she brought him around a lot –

ANNE. Her son was in the class?

MARK. No. No. She was in the class. She was interested in signing her son up for the kiddie class – it doesn't matter. She was in my class. He was not. He was nine.

ANNE. Okay…

MARK. The reason I'm upset is because she hasn't been to class for a few weeks. So I called to find out what happened. And what I found out was, tonight, was… Her husband lives in Philadelphia and the son was visiting the father over the weekend, and there was some kind of a drive-by shooting, and her little boy was shot to death –

ANNE. Oh my God.

MARK. – outside a movie theater in Philadelphia. And I was very upset to hear about it because I got to know him a little this year –

ANNE. Oh my God, of course.

MARK. – and I was just a bit shocked to hear about it. She's a wreck of course. She wants to kill herself, but she's Catholic, so she's afraid that she would go to hell and then she would never see him again. Which of course she never will anyway.

ANNE. When did this happen?

MARK. Three weeks ago.

ANNE. How well do you know them?

MARK. Not very well. She would stick around after class for a few minutes. The son was very interested in astronomy.

ANNE. Well, God. I'm sorry…

MARK. …In any case, I didn't really know how to end the conversation.

ANNE. No, God, of course not…

MARK. And then the driving was incredible. It took me literally an hour just to get out of Manhattan…

ANNE. God…

MARK. I didn't mean to snap at you. (*Pause*)

ANNE. Listen. I've been thinking about this all week.

MARK. Yes?

ANNE. I want you to take that job. I know –

MARK (*starts to speak*). –

ANNE. Now just wait a minute. I've really thought about this. I want you to take that job. If we have to cut back we have to cut back. As long as it doesn't affect Adam's college. But I want you to try it because – When we met, you wanted to be an astronomer. And then you decided that everybody you were working with was more talented than you…

MARK. That's not exactly –

ANNE. Yes you did. You told me that. And I never forgot it. It was the most terrible thing I ever heard anybody say about themselves.

MARK. There's nothing terrible about it. Not everybody is equally good at all the same things.

ANNE. And I don't like the way you run around telling people that Adam is not that talented at music.

MARK. He's not. At least not in my amateur opinion. It's not an insult.

ANNE. I don't like you saying it. I don't like the way you say it. I don't like you lumping him in with your own defeated miserable opinion of yourself. I know you don't feel that way all the time, and it's certainly not what *I* think of you, but I don't think it's right for you to go around telling people he's not that talented. Maybe he is and maybe he isn't. But I think there's something wrong with your saying it. We're supposed to prop him up and help him and encourage him, not tear him down and diminish his expectations of himself before he gets a chance to get started. I don't mean he should be a musician, or even wants to be. But why give him such a limited expectation of himself from the start, Mark? He'll find out about himself in time. I know you think a happy childhood is a lousy preparation for life –

MARK. It does create a certain set of false expectations.

ANNE. Yeah, and if nobody encourages you then you have *no* expectations. What's so great about *that*? I think he should know when he grows up and he does have a hard time that *somebody* thinks he's great, and that's supposed to be us!

MARK. I do think he's great.

ANNE. Yeah, but you gotta act like it! It's not funny to make that joke all the time. And I don't like you making it about yourself! You're a *wonderful* teacher. You think that's shit? I don't. But if you want to get back into astronomy so badly, I think it would be a life-destroying mistake not to try. And if the job is a humiliating bore, then okay: You tried it. But maybe that's not the reason for any of this.

MARK. Any of what.

ANNE. Why I've been waiting for the last six months for you to tell me you don't want to be married to me anymore…!

MARK. What are you talking about?

ANNE. Well you come home every night and it's just so obvious you don't want to be here…! And you don't say anything, so I've just been waiting…!

MARK. That's not true, Anne.

ANNE. Maybe you're just sick of me.

MARK. I'm not sick of you. I've just been sick of everything.

ANNE. I would assume that includes me. It's not totally unheard of. I'm sure getting sick of you.

MARK (*a joke:*). I can't believe *that*…

ANNE. But I still love you. Very much. Do you still love me?

MARK. Of course I do. Of course I do. And I appreciate your saying all that. But I honestly don't see how we can do it. And it's not because I'm being defeatist –

ANNE. I didn't – I don't mean 'defeatist' –

The doorbell rings.

There they are! (*Ironically.*) 'Yay…!'

MARK. Now, we're sleeping on the sofa, is that right?

ANNE. God, that is another really funny joke. Would you get Adam please?

ANNE *exits.* MARK *goes to the stairs and calls up.*

MARK. Adam? Adam!

ADAM (*off*). Yeah?

Offstage we hear a group 'Hi! 'Oh my God, we were getting so worried!' 'Here we are, finally!' 'Hello!' 'Hi, Eleanor! You remember Rob,' etc.

MARK. Your grandmother's here…! Come and say hello.

ADAM (*off*). Be right down.

MARK. Now I hope you don't mind. They're all staying in your room.

ADAM (*off*). I hate to tell you this, Dad, but you've made that joke like five times this week already.

MARK. I'm refining it.

ADAM (*off*). Har-dee-har-har.

ANNE (*off*). Mark! Adam! Come say hi!

MARK. We're coming!

He takes a few sharp breaths and leans heavily against the wall. Under the following he has a complete silent breakdown of utter despair.

ANNE (*off*). Mark! Adam! Come say hi! Now Mom, you and Eleanor are gonna be upstairs. Eleanor it's the second door on the left, right up the stairs. Rob you're right in there. Do you guys have a lot of luggage?

ANNE'S MOM, ELEANOR *and* ROB (*off*). Oh no, just a couple of bags. My gosh, it is really coming down out there…! (*Etc.*)

ANNE (*off*). Mark…!

MARK *straightens himself up.*

MARK. Yes. Be right there!

He gets ahold of himself.

(*Calling up the stairs.*) Adam? Come on, buddy. It's not so bad.

ADAM (*off*). I'm afraid that's where you and I will have to disagree, Dad.

Scene Seven

Crossfade to NORMAN*'s hospital room.* NORMAN *is sitting up in a chair, still hooked up to IVs, but looking a lot better.* DORIS *is sitting across from him.*

DORIS. Apparently her husband was involved with some gang in Philadelphia? Anyway. Horrible.

NORMAN. That's not what Rowena said. But it's still horrible.

DORIS. How are you feeling?

NORMAN. I feel okay.

DORIS. You had us a little worried there...!

NORMAN. Yes I know.

DORIS. Welcome back.

NORMAN. Thanks sweetheart.

She gets tearful and bends over the bed to hug him. After a moment she straightens up.

DORIS. I'm gonna go. I'll see you bright and early.

NORMAN. Okay.

DORIS. I love you.

NORMAN. Okay, me too.

DORIS. Oh. I was waiting to tell you this – your garage called...

ANGELA *comes in.*

ANGELA. Oh – I'm sorry –

DORIS. Oh that's all right, Angela, come in. I was leaving in a second.

ANGELA. I could come back.

DORIS. No no no, come in.

NORMAN. Come in, Angela.

ANGELA. I just heard the good news...!

DORIS. Yes. Thank you. Please come in.

ANGELA. Hi Norman!

NORMAN. Hello sweetheart.

ANGELA. Denise says you're going home tomorrow!

NORMAN. Can you believe it?

ANGELA. I'm so happy for you Norman...!

NORMAN. Thank you honey.

ANGELA. I been away the last few weeks, so I didn't know how you were doing...

NORMAN. I know. They told us about your son.

DORIS. Yes. Maureen told us about it yesterday. I am so sorry, Angela...

ANGELA. Thank you.

NORMAN. I don't understand why you're here.

ANGELA. I just want to get back to work. I can't sit around all day.

DORIS. Well we want you to know, if there's anything we can do, please let us know.

ANGELA. Thank you, Doris.

DORIS. All right. I was on my way out.

NORMAN. What were you going to ask me about?

DORIS. Oh. I don't remember. (*Pause*) Huh. I can't remember. Your car – ? We'll talk about it later. I'll see you in the morning. And I mean it, Angela, if there's anything we can do, just let us know.

ANGELA. Like what? (*Pause*)

DORIS. I don't know. Legal help. Or... I don't know.

ANGELA. No – there's nothing else to do. That's it.

DORIS. All right. Well... needless to say, the last time I saw you... I was very overwrought... I think we were all a little crazy the last few weeks.

ANGELA. Thank you.

DORIS. Anyway… we've got Dad back. That's all I really care about. The two of you can get married, for all I care, as long as we've got him back.

NORMAN. What the fuck are you talking about? Who'm I getting married to?

DORIS. Nobody, I hope! For their sake.

NORMAN. Oh, well, thank you.

DORIS. Anyway – I'm so sorry about David…

NORMAN. Stop telling her that.

DORIS. Well I am!

NORMAN. She doesn't give a fuck if we're sorry. Stop saying that.

DORIS (*very embarrassed*). Hey, give me a break, okay?

NORMAN. Would you go home, Doris?

DORIS. Yes. I am. Gee! I guess things are really getting back to normal around here…!

NORMAN. Just go home. You can't make her feel better. Just go away.

DORIS. Thank you, Dad!

NORMAN. Oh stop suffering!

DORIS. You know what? I liked you better when you were dying.

As DORIS *exits:*

NORMAN. Everybody did.

DORIS *exits.*

ANGELA. I gotta go home. (*Pause*) I'm so happy you're alive…!

NORMAN. Thank you honey.

She starts crying.

ANGELA. I don't know what I'm gonna do…!

NORMAN. I don't either.

ANGELA. I don't understand what happened…!

She sits in the bed next to his chair. He reaches out for her hand.
She gets up and hugs him. He can't sit up so well, so this
requires her stooping way over the chair.

NORMAN. Nobody does, honey. You don't have to understand it.

ANGELA. They put me on tranquilizers, but they're making me
crazy. I can't take them any more. I been going to church every
day. My mother and my sister go with me. Raymond won't go
with me. He moved back in with me last week, but he's sleeping
on the sofa. I told him I want to get married. But he won't even
come with me to church… Norman, I gotta tell you something,
because I can't tell anybody else. I told my confessor, but…
I was seeing somebody. He was married. It was this really weird
thing. I was seeing him, like sending David to my mother's or to
Juanita's, and then he would come over. And when David went
to Philadelphia on the weekends I used to see him on Friday
nights. I didn't tell anybody. Nobody knows about it. But this
guy was married and they had a son. And the weekend he died
I sent David to Philadelphia so I could see this guy… and that's
when they shot him. And I told Father Bernal about it right away
when David died, because I couldn't believe God would take
David away because of what I was doing. But then I kept
thinking how you're always saying 'Look in the paper: what do
you think God is doing to all those poor people in Bosnia, or all
those little kids on the second floor.' Remember?

NORMAN. Sure.

ANGELA. And I said, 'You don't get it, Norman.' Remember?
I told you, 'God loves them too: we just don't understand.' And
you got really mad at me, remember?

NORMAN. I remember.

ANGELA. So I told Father Bernal everything you said. And he
said…

NORMAN. What?

ANGELA. He said God didn't kill David. The sin killed David.

NORMAN. The what?

ANGELA. The sin. He said the sin killed David. He said that David
was with God, and I was with my sin. And when I gave up my

sin I would be with God again too. He said that to me two days
after David died. I been going to pray in church every day. But
when I think about –

NORMAN. Oh honey –

ANGELA. No, let me talk! If I think about what he told me,
I swear to God it's like it makes me feel like I'm gonna throw
up. Like I get sick to my stomach when I think about it. Because
I know it's true. Don't argue with me yet! But I can't argue with
him. And I can't tell my family what I did, and I couldn't tell
Raymond. That's why I want to talk to you. My girlfriends love
me, but they're just kids. You know: They're just like me. They
don't know anything.

NORMAN. Nobody knows anything. And I don't believe in God.

ANGELA. I know you don't, that's why I want to talk to you – !

NORMAN. Wait a minute. There's nothing you can do about this.
You better face that fact first. That's all I can tell you. I'm
seventy-two years old. There's nothing you can do about this
and that priest is not your friend. I don't give a fuck how you
look at it. He's not your friend. You don't need to talk to him. If
you need to talk to a priest, go find one with some humility. Go
find one who believes that human beings are more important
than his rotten ideas. That David was just as important as you
are. That there are reasons he got killed, that have to do with
why there are gangs of kids driving around shooting out the
window, but none of them have to do with the fact that you got
yourself a married boyfriend. That may be wrong and it may not
be. I don't happen to give a shit about stuff like that, but some
people do. But they can go to hell if they think it's any kind of
justice to murder David because his mother was getting laid. Or
because she was lonely. That's not justice, it's venom. It's some
kind of sexual rage, or I don't know what. But it comes from a
different part of people. I don't go for that. And I don't want you
talking to anybody who goes for that right now.

ANGELA. Oh Norman. I can't get up in the morning. I don't want
to be a nurse anymore. I don't want to do anything. I just want to
die so I can see my little boy again.

NORMAN. There's plenty of time for that, Angela. There's plenty
of time for that.

Scene Eight

Crossfade to MARK*'s classroom.* MARK *stands alone, waiting for a long moment.* IAN *comes in.*

IAN. Hello.

MARK. Hello.

IAN. Last class…!

MARK. Yes.

IAN. So do you think you'd have a few minutes after class? For part two?

He waves a yellow document at MARK.

MARK. Um…

IAN. It's not finished obviously.

MARK. Oh no?

IAN. Well, there's still one class. So usually what I do is I'll just give a verbal summation, based on whatever impressions I get from the final session.

MARK. I see.

IAN. But then a lot of times I'll deliver a final appraisal at the last class, and then I'll just go home and totally re-evaluate the whole thing in like a few days. So don't be surprised if you get another totally different written critique from me in the mail like in a week or two.

MARK. I'll try not to be.

IAN. Huh. You play it pretty close to the vest, huh?

MARK. Do I?

IAN. No, I like that. I like that… But… interesting. (*Pause*)

MARK. Who are you?

IAN. I don't get you.

MARK. What are you? What do you do the rest of the time? Where are your parents? What are you?

IAN. Wow.

MARK. I don't mean that cruelly. I'm – baffled.

IAN. No, I, um… I live in the East Village… I'm from Hanover
New Hampshire… I work at Kinko's. (*Becoming self-conscious.*)
I take a lot of classes… Um, this one. Journalism. Poli-sci. Far
Eastern Studies. Animal psychology…

MARK. Really.

IAN. Why limit yourself? It's a big old world.

MRS PYSNER *comes in.*

MARK. Hello.

She takes her seat without answering.

IAN. …. Welding. That was kind of tough. I'm not very good with
my hands.

MARK. We should get a move on…

IAN. Looking forward to it. (*Waves his yellow booklet.*) Don't blow
it! Just kidding. I'm tough but fair.

MARK. Shall we get started?

IAN *takes his seat. The lights shift. It's the end of the class.*

Well. As you know, this was our last class together. I hope you
found it stimulating and, uh, illuminating… The Planetarium
does offer several more advanced astronomy classes, for which
I trust you are all now fully qualified… As many of you may
also know, this was also the last class I or anyone will teach in
this classroom. The new Planetarium starts construction after the
New Year. Regular classes will continue of course, in the
Museum of Natural History, next door, but I think it might be
appropriate to say a word or two in the few minutes remaining to
us. Many New Yorkers – and those of us who live in the
environs – have a very warm feeling for this building. Just as
many children have their favourite animals in the zoo. Or just as
some of us have our favorite paintings in the museum. It may
not be the best painting in the collection, but it's the one for
which we have a special feeling. Or affinity. The one we go right
in to look at whenever we visit the museum. So it's with a great

feeling of sadness that I personally say farewell to the Hayden
Planetarium. When the case was being made for tearing it down,
it was frequently characterized as being somewhat stuffy, and
institutional. I would have to take a strong exception to that.
I think it's a beautiful little building, with a wonderful
atmosphere. One that somehow captures something of the
mystery and the sense of awe, on a greatly reduced scale of
course, that most people feel when contemplating the heavens.
Or the motion of the spheres, as it used to be called... The
beautiful marble steps, a little too wide, or too deep, to walk up
and down comfortably... But which are so much fun to race up
and down when you're a youngster... The handsome black
marble... and the wonderful wide chrome banisters that you
can't quite get your hand around... But for those of us who grew
up straining our necks around in those wonderful cushioned
bucket seats, looking around to find out where that seemingly
all-knowing, slightly pedantic voice echoing over the address
system was coming from... it seemed like a wonderful peek
behind the curtain to discover this formal, dull little fellow,
behind a little lectern, wearing glasses and a suit, tucked away in
a back corner of the auditorium. His face is lit from below,
dimly, like the conductor of a symphony orchestra; lit from
below by a mysterious light... But what I'll miss most is
something I suppose no one will ever see again. It's the moment
before the show starts, when you go inside. It's dim in the Sky
Theater but not yet dark. And the marvelous Zeiss 6 projector is
not projecting the stars on the big dome: It's projecting a
beautiful three-hundred-and-sixty-degree view of the buildings
around Central Park. The great dome overhead is a purplish
color. There's music playing, and then the color in the sky fades
away. And as this happens, lights go on in all the windows of all
the buildings around the Park, faintly at first... but then the Zeiss
6 slowly brings out the stars overhead, just as they would begin
to appear in a real sunset. Then the Sky Show starts and the
buildings fade out altogether. And you suddenly see the night
sky in all its glory. What I always liked about this way of
starting every show, was that it placed *you*, the visitor, right in
the picture. We *are* on 81st Street and Central Park West, in New
York City, right across the street from Central Park. The
projected buildings are the very same ones we would see if we
went outside. And on our tiny little dome, the stars and nebulae

and planets projected by our wonderful machine really do resemble the real thing, countless millions of miles over our heads, but brighter and more fascinating, more mysterious and more real than anything any of us ever dreamt of in our wildest imaginings. I'm not a religious man, but as I grow older I am more and more aware of a thin, inadequate feeling that grows and grows as you cling to your total rejection of mysticism and the fantastic – when all life is more fantastic than imagination allows. It's such thin gruel. But don't our testable beliefs have to mean something? Don't they have to stand up on their own merits against the demands of our wishes, and the deficits in our imagination? I think they do. But it leaves us so horribly and infinitely cold and alone. But that's why I like the opera, or some opera anyway. Because the opera treats every human life as a tremendous event, a gigantic drama, something of monumental importance. Which is why opera is ridiculous, and why it's true. (*Pause*) In any case, I certainly hope you've enjoyed the course. I've certainly enjoyed teaching it. It's a great privilege to be able to look up at the night sky and know with a reasonable degree of certainty what it is we're actually looking at. These things are not easy to figure out. Our ancestors thought the stars were fixed to enormous crystal spheres, and they were no dumber than we are. But they chipped away and chipped away, and because of what they did, now we know something about what's really up there. I'm not an astronomer… but I'm a part of astronomy too. Because I *am* that little man behind the podium. I get to deliver the news. I'm the messenger. Some of you may think it's not much of an ambition, but I can honestly say that from the age of seven, when my wonderful parents first brought me to the Planetarium, it's the only place I ever really wanted to be. So the next time you find yourself looking at the sky at night –

MRS PYSNER (*raising her hand*). Question?

MARK. If you could just… Um – Yes.

MRS PYSNER. Yeah… Can you explain the difference between a galaxy and a solar system again?

MARK. Yes. A – our Solar System consists of a star – our Sun – which is orbited by planets, like the Earth. A galaxy is a formation of stars, gas and dust. And somewhere in there is the so-called 'missing' or 'dark' mass that makes up approximately ninety-two percent of the known mass of the universe, and which remains to be –

MRS PYSNER. The what?

MARK. But which is a difficult topic, probably more suitable…

MRS PYSNER. Dark mass?

MARK. – more suitable for the intermediate course. Which I sincerely hope you will all sign up for…! And, uh, well, that's it. Thank you very much.

The class applauds politely. MARK *starts gathering his materials.* MRS PYSNER *puts her coat on, walks past* MARK *without saying anything and exits.* IAN *comes up to* MARK *with the yellow report in hand. Pause.*

IAN. *Much* better.

MARK *is startled, then pleased, then he blushes.*

MARK. Oh, well…

IAN. You know what? I wanna mail this to you. It may be a few days.

MARK. Take your time. And, uh, thank you, Ian. I appreciate um, the input…

MARK *sees that* ANGELA *has slipped in the doorway.*

IAN. Yeah. I just had a couple of questions I wanted to ask you if that's okay. You were talking about –

MARK. Ian, I'm going to have to interrupt you. I'm sorry.

IAN. I'll be really quick.

MARK. Why don't you call me, or drop by. I'll be more than happy to answer anything you want to ask me, but I'm really going to have to ask you to excuse me. (*Pause*)

IAN. All right.

MARK. But thanks again for your input. I really do appreciate it.

IAN. Yeah. Everyone appreciates it but no one wants to hear it.

MARK. Good luck.

IAN. Okay, same to you.

MARK *offers his hand.* IAN *shakes it and exits.*

ANGELA. Sorry…

MARK. Don't be sorry. I'm so glad to see you.

ANGELA. You are?

MARK. Of course I am!

He goes to her and puts his arms around her. She hugs him back.

I'm expecting Anne. But do you want to get a…

ANGELA. That's okay. I only got a minute… I'm sorry I never called you back…

MARK. Oh no, you didn't have to call me back…

ANGELA. No, but thank you for your messages. They were really sweet.

MARK. I'm very glad you came by.

ANGELA. Yeah, me too. (*Pause*)

MARK. How is Raymond doing?

ANGELA. Not so good. He was staying with me for a while, but I made him move out.

MARK. Oh?

ANGELA. Yeah. It was too hard to be around him. I wanted him to see a doctor but he won't do anything. He just goes to the cemetery all the time. I don't know what's gonna happen to him. But he won't let me do anything for him.

MARK. Do you still think you're going to get married?

ANGELA. No, everybody says that's nuts. That's not gonna bring him back. It's obviously crazy…

MARK. Well, it seems to me there's no rush. If that's what you end up doing… you can always do it later.

ANGELA. Yeah, that's what everybody says. (*Pause*) It's never gonna get better…!

MARK. Maybe not. But it won't always be like this.

She starts crying. MARK puts his arms around her. ANNE steps into the doorway and sees them. After a moment she withdraws. ANGELA pulls away and wipes her eyes.

ANGELA. I went up to five nights a week on the nursing program. It keeps me really busy. So I'm gonna finish early.

MARK. Oh, that's good.

ANGELA. For a while I thought I was gonna quit. But I think it's really good for me. It's good to see you're not the only one with problems.

MARK. Of course...

ANGELA. But I want to say I really miss you. I been thinking about you. I know I said a lot of things to you...

MARK. No no, that's all right...

ANGELA. – but I know you care about me. You're the only one that treats me like a grown-up. And I am a grown-up. Anyway, I'll be around if you want to call me. I'll call you back.

MARK. I can call you tomorrow.

ANGELA. Okay, that'd be great.

She kisses him quickly and hurries out. MARK goes to his desk and starts packing his materials. ARNOLD comes in.

ARNOLD. Hey, do you know Anne is here?

MARK. No. How long has she been here?

ARNOLD. I don't know. She's in the hall.

MARK goes to the doorway.

MARK. She's not there now.

ARNOLD. She's probably in the bathroom. Listen, I wanted to tell you: I talked to Herschel this morning... I had him call the college for you.

MARK. Oh.

ARNOLD. Yeah. I told him your situation, and he called them up and yelled at them and now they're gonna try to work it out.

MARK. I don't believe it.

ANNE *comes in.*

ARNOLD. It's all true. They're supposedly gonna call you tomorrow.

ANNE. What's all true?

MARK. Hello. Arnold just…

ARNOLD. I was just telling your husband that I got Herschel Moritz to call City College and be famous and bully them into figuring out Mark's schedule so he can take the job with Ben and Herschel.

ANNE. You're kidding.

ARNOLD. No.

MARK. But how can they do it? They told me it was impossible.

ARNOLD. I don't know. They told him they would. He's very famous.

MARK. Arnold… I can't believe it.

ARNOLD. Plus I told Herschel you were really interested in moving into other areas of the project eventually, and he said he figured as much. So if you hang in there for a year or two it sounds like he's probably gonna move you up.

MARK. Arnold…!

ANNE. Arnold…!

ARNOLD. So welcome back! You've actually effected a return to Academia. A virtually unheard-of feat. Anyway, gotta run. Good to see you, Anne.

ANNE. Yeah, you too.

MARK *shakes hands with* ARNOLD.

MARK. Merry Christmas, Arnold. I honestly don't know how to thank you.

ARNOLD. Well, you've got the rest of your life to work it out. See you in January. (*Generally.*) Goodbye, Planetarium.

ARNOLD *goes out.*

MARK. Can you believe that?

ANNE. No, I can't...

They look at each other. Silence.

MARK. Where's Adam?

ANNE. He's in the car. I'm double parked. Everybody's at the restaurant.

MARK. I'm sorry. I didn't realize. Just give me one second.

MARK *starts to pack up his stuff.* ANNE *watches him.*

ANNE. So – it turns out you can have everything. (*Pause*)

MARK. Yes. I can have everything...

Pause. He resumes packing his stuff up as the lights fade out.

The End.

www.nickhernbooks.co.uk

facebook.com/nickhernbooks

twitter.com/nickhernbooks